The **TEEN**

Business Manual

A guide for Teen Leadership & Entrepreneurship

BY JAMES SCOTT

NEW RENAISSANCE
CORPORATION

DISCLAIMER AND/OR LEGAL NOTICES

About the Author

James Scott is a consultant, "7 Time Best Selling Author" and lecturer on the topics of Cybersecurity and corporate strategy. Mr. Scott has authored multiple books such as: The CEO's Manual on Cyber Security, The Book on Mergers and Acquisitions, Taking Your Company Public: A Corporate Strategies Manual, The CEO Manual 4 Kids, The Book on Healthcare IT: What you need to know about HIPAA, Hospital IT and Healthcare Information Technology , The Book on PPMs: Regulation D 504 Edition, The Book on PPMs: Regulation D 505 Edition, The Book on PPMs: Regulation D 506 Edition as well as several templates that make the process of completing complicated S1 and PPM docs as easy as 'point and click' for entrepreneurs and corporate CEOs.

Mr. Scott is a member of several economic think tanks that study diverse aspects of legislation concepts that effect corporations worldwide such as: Aspen Institute, Chatham House: Royal Institute of International Affairs, The American Enterprise Institute, Economic Research Council, American Institute for Economic Research, The Manhattan Institute and The Hudson Institute among others.

To contact James Scott visit the 'Contact Us' page at the New Renaissance Corporation publishing website at: **newrenaissancecorporation.com**

Contents

Preface

Powerful, dynamic CEOs aren't born that way; they are carefully nurtured and sculpted. Even the Jack Welches and Bill Gates' of the world were once just motivated kids looking for the tools they needed to fulfill their dreams and turn their ideas into reality. Too often, adults dismiss the natural skills and "out-of-the-box" business ideas of youth, simply because of the entrepreneur's age. America needs to stop and take note of these up-and-coming business titans and give them the encouragement and training they need to rise to their full potential.

In 1976, 16-year-old Steve Jobs, along with Steve Wozniak and Ronald Wayne, founded Apple Computer in Jobs' parents' garage. That collaboration would eventually launch the Macintosh computer, iTunes, the iPod, the iPad and other devices that have become all, but essential to the way we live. In 2005, "People" magazine called Jobs the "Father of the Digital Age."

More recently, Mark Zuckerberg was just 19 years old when he launched what would become Facebook in his Harvard University dorm room in 2003. By age 23, Zuckerberg was a billionaire and named by "Time" magazine as one of the wealthiest and most influential men in the world. His creation now helps more than one billion individuals and businesses interact with one another and has changed the way the world communicates.

Jobs and Zuckerberg aren't isolated examples. In 2010, "Inc." magazine profiled 10 teenagers whose ideas and leadership have earned them at least $1 million. These included a 17-year-old who sold his mobile news app to Yahoo! for $30 million and a teen whose online furniture business, started in his bedroom when he was just 14 years old, is now reported to be worth more than $40 million. Fastupfront.com talks about other teen entrepreneurs, like a 14-year-old Brit with a passion for fruit jam, who started a company that now grosses more than 1.2 million in annual sales, and a teen from the south side of Chicago, who became the world's youngest self-made millionaire (outside of the entertainment industry) at age 14 and is now a motivational speaker and author.

The role of entrepreneurs in the United States

According to the U.S. Department of Labor, the more than 25 million small businesses in the United States provide more than half of the private sector jobs in the U.S., generate more than half of the country's gross national product and are the prime source for new jobs in America. The role of small businesses and the entrepreneurs who run them cannot be overstated.

Why cultivating young entrepreneurs is important

A 2005 U.S. Department of Labor study found that more than two-thirds of American teenagers want to become entrepreneurs. Despite this desire, there are few training courses available in schools about entrepreneurship as a career path. Yet, young entrepreneurship is on the rise. According to a study by the Kaufman Foundation, 29 percent of new entrepreneurial activity in 2011 was by individuals between 20 and 34 years of age. However, young business leaders face a host of challenges their older competitors don't have to deal with, such as not being taken seriously by financial backers and even customers and potential employees.

Encouraging the next generation of business leaders has never been more important. As business becomes more global--and more competitive--we need the best and brightest minds at work for America. That means encouraging the dreams of our young men and women and making the tools they need to succeed available to them. Parents, teachers and business professionals all need to do their part.

And, teens don't have to be the next Bill Gates to benefit from entrepreneurial training. According to a study by the National Foundation for Teaching Entrepreneurship, such education increased participants' interest in attending college (by 32 percent), helped to promote independent reading, increased interest in their occupational aspirations and promoted the belief that attaining one's goal is within a person's control.

About this book

If you're a kid with a big dream, we think you'll find the information here exciting and helpful to starting you on the path to fulfilling your dream and turning your idea into a concrete, money-making entity. We talk about basic issues like types of capital, how to write an effective press release and the types of stock as well as more complex topics like how to take your company public, leadership skills and basic crisis management.

Realizing your dream of starting your own company has never been more attainable. Organizations like the U.S. Small Business Administration have put together programs to encourage young, motivated business men and women and to help them receive the funding they need to take that next step.

We understand that starting out in the business world can be scary as well as exciting. We want you to give you some of the tools you'll need so you can take those wonderful ideas of yours and soar with them. Who knows? You might just have that germ of an idea that will become the next Facebook or Apple Computer.

Chapter 1
Great Leadership Qualities

Excellent leadership qualities do not come naturally to many, but those who do have them are usually very successful business people. Just because you know how to give instructions, that doesn't make you a good leader. You have to be able to communicate with your staff, keep high morale within your company, commit to your team and business, have a good attitude and mix in some great instinct.

Additionally, you should have a good sense of humor to mix into the batch, and you should have plenty of self-assurance. Without the right combination, you may not be able to get through to your staff; and your business will suffer.

Be a Good Communicator

You may know what you want to tell your staff, but while you are explaining a thought process, some of your employees will look at you with a blank stare. Big Fat Problem. Your business cannot be effective if you cannot communicate your wishes to your staff. Furthermore, poor communication leads to bad morale and high staff turnover – at the least. You could have a low staff turnover, but lose customers because an unhappy staff projects its low morale to customers. Once a customer receives poor treatment or comes to the conclusion that the employees are not happy, that customer may not return.

A customer may not return if he or she thinks you are treating your employees roughly, simply because that customer does not want to support someone who does not respect and trust his or her staff and employees.

If you do get blank stares or notice that employees can't seem to do anything right, the issue may be with your communication skills. To run a successful business, you must be able to succinctly and clearly describe your needs. When you are able to do this, you and your staff will be able to work toward the same goal – you will be able to work as a team.

When your communication skills are top notch, you should be able to easily train your team to be productive and friendly. To help with communication, you should have an open door policy and be available to staff throughout the day. Holding a daily meeting – either in the morning or just before everyone goes home – to discuss any issues also leads to better communication. Your staff needs to know that it can go to you with problems that they cannot handle on their own. The staff also needs to know that you are confident enough to sort the problems out in an effective manner.

Once your staff and employees knows they can trust you to lead them in the right direction and that you are adept at handling whatever comes your way, they will be more apt to work harder and to work as a well-oiled machine.

Have a Sense of Humor

The first thing you think of doing when something goes wrong is to scream and yell. These actions will make your staff very unhappy and they will dread coming to work. If a staff member makes a mistake, surely speak to him or her about it and discuss how to keep that mistake from happening again.

In your discussion, keep your tone even and you can even import your sense of humor once you know the staff member understands how to keep from making the same mistake. With excellent communication, you should have hardly any staff errors.

If something happens that is beyond the control of you or your staff member, such as a web site crash or a lost customer due to circumstances beyond your control, treat the situation with a little levity and a sense of humor. Once your staff realizes that you are not going to blow a head gasket every time something goes wrong, they will not be afraid to come to you regarding a potential issue.

If someone comes to you when that person realizes that the company is going to be in the weeds, you might be able to head the problem off before it happens. Excellent communication between you and your staff and between staff members, along with a little humor, can often stop issues before they bury you.

Be Self-Assured

Self-assurance is important when things are not going right – and things will not always be peachy when you own a business. There are times when your brand may come under fire – whether your business is large or small -- because of something a V.I.P. customer says or because of a problem with manufacturing. Stocks may drop and you may see a decline in customers.

It is at this point that you should have a high confidence level and a calm demeanor. When you are calm during a situation, you import that calmness to your staff. This allows them to work confidently and to help restore your brand image. As a business owner or manager, part of your job is to put out the fires that may appear from time to time. If you can fight the fire with confidence and keep your wits about you, your staff will be more responsive, thus extinguishing the flames that much sooner.

Making a Commitment

A hard-working team and having quality content means that you work with your team. In addition to management, you also help your staff with their jobs. When your staff and employees see you working hard to make the business work, they also work hard. When you prove your commitment to your brand, your staff and employees will follow suit. When things go wrong – and they will – your staff will back you up and help with damage control. When things are going well, your staff will chip in to make things go even better.

Commitment also means keeping promises. Whether the promise is to your staff, a vendor or a customer, never go back on your word. Keeping promises boosts team morale and shows customers and vendors that they can trust you. It also boosts your reputation as a fair business person.

When you make and keep promises to your staff and employees, they won't make promises to customers and vendors that they can't keep – employees always follow their boss's examples and actions. Your business will become known as an honest business if you keep it honest with your staff and employees.

Have an Optimistic Attitude

A motivated team is the key to a successful business. Excellent communication skills, working alongside your staff and bonuses keep everyone on an even keel. Depending on the size of your operation, you may provide "extras" for your staff – you may have a water cooler, a well-stocked coffee center, and a small kitchen with a microwave so people can heat up meals, popcorn and hot drinks.

A break room with a kitchen area also gives the staff an informal place to meet for chit-chat or to get advice and help with a project. You might even provide snacks for the employees. You can get things like pretzels and popcorn in bulk. If everyone has the ability to run to the kitchen for a quick snack, their energy levels stay up, and staff morale is high. Remember the old saying "All work and no play..." That applies to you, your staff and your employees. Having a place to take a break from the office makes employees move around and see something other than the four same walls. It may even encourage new ideas – just because of a "change in scenery."

You may even provide beer for those who would like to hang out after work and talk to co-workers about their job or life in general. Providing extras for the staff may seem like small thing, but it shows your employees that you care about them.

You could also set up a bonus system. Whether it is for the person with the highest sales or because someone went over and above in their job duties during the past month, employees always enjoy a surprise bonus. Just be sure to follow through with the bonus system – don't do it for a couple of months, then can the program.

Getting People to Contribute – Including You

If you contribute after hours when you need to, your staff will be more willing to help after hours to keep a customer happy or to finish a report needed the next morning. Furthermore, if the staff and employees see that you put in extra time, they will be more willing to do their best to make sure deadlines are met and customers are happy. When you have a hard-working staff, you have a recipe for success.

It is difficult to ask a staff member or employee to do something that you wouldn't do yourself. If the after-hours job takes two or three people, don't ask the entire staff to stay – ask a couple of people to help you. Remember, the more hands you have and the more brains you have, the faster the work will go – unless you have too many: Then it seems to take three times as long to complete a project because extra people just get in the way.

Use Your Imagination

Sometimes you may be forced to veer onto a side road because of unforeseen circumstances. This usually happens when you have a fire to put out or when someone -- usually a customer – doesn't follow the game plan.

When you come up on a problem, use your imagination to come up with a good solution. Involve your staff in deciding the best path to take to get the business – or the customer – back on track. For example, if you are in marketing and you created an over-the-top marketing campaign for a new customer, but the customer hates the idea; you'll have to come up with something else rather quickly or you may lose the account. This is the best time to get all of your staff involved, even those that are not working on that particular campaign. Fresh brains may be able to come up with fresh ideas, and more importantly, the one fresh idea that your customer loves.

Furthermore, it gives you an opportunity to see which employees have additional skills that you may use. You may have just found your next top-notch marketer. Just because someone is in the mail room doesn't mean they don't have excellent ideas. That person may have no self-confidence, but given the chance can really show off. This is an excellent time to boost this employee's morale.

If you are put into a situation where you have to make a choice and both options are bad choices, be sure you think both options through completely – don't make a bad situation worse by making an emotional decision on the fly. Once you've made a decision, ask your staff to punch holes in it – find the bad things about that decision. They may think of something you missed – and the staff will know that you trust them enough to help make a hard decision. If both decisions are not good for the company, but you must make one, choose the decision with the least amount of consequences – as long as it's a moral avenue.

Use Your Instinct

Eventually, no matter how much experience you have with running a business, you are going to come across a new and different situation. You won't have a roadmap and will have to make decisions on the fly. In addition, the riskier the decision, the more pressure you'll have – not just on you, but on your staff, too.

You can use past experiences that are similar to help you through the decision-making process or you can ask your staff for suggestions. No matter how you make the decision – even with your staff's assistance – you need to guide the staff through the process. Your employees trust you to make the right decision for the company.

Following your instinct and using your natural intuition also helps guide you through a rough time. You can also reach out to your mentors and advisory board for support. Regardless of what anyone suggests, the final decision is up to you – and you will be the one to come to the ultimate decision of what is best for your brand reputation. Once you learn to trust yourself as your employees do, some of these decisions will be easier.

Always Inspire Others

Inspiration is always good, especially if the business is new and off to a slow start. Most businesses do have a rough time the first two or three years and often take a loss. Inspire your team to work through the tough times by ensuring they can see the success that will come because of hard work. Whether you are working with partners or you have a staff that you depend on to get you through the day, all team members must be on board.

You can generate enthusiasm by setting and reviewing smaller, weekly or monthly goals. If you use a three- or five-year goal, it may seem like you aren't getting anything done. However, if you set short-term goals, everyone sees progress and will be more willing to get through the tough times. It's almost like telling yourself, "Ten more yards and I'm halfway through the marathon – I can do it!" Keep a dry-erase board in the kitchen so all employees know where to find the goal status.

If energy levels are falling because of hard work or low morale, give your staff – and yourself – a break. Be sure to tell everyone they are doing a great job and knock off a few hours early or take some time for an office party.

Have Integrity

Even if your ethical values are high, you need to hold your business to higher ethical values. Remember, your team and your business are a reflection of you, thus if your business is highly ethical, you are, too. Ethical values tie in with keeping high employee morale and happy customers. Your employees will have the same values as you, so you must "lead the pack" when it comes down to making ethical choices.

Be a Contributor

When you planned your business, you had a vision of what it would take to make it successful. Certain values and core beliefs fit into that success. To ensure a smooth-running operation, you may want to create a list of core beliefs and values; and post them for all employees to see.

At the same time, be sure to encourage openness in the office – this is part of your communication skills. If your employees know your values, they will be influenced by those values when they see you sticking to them. They will also be more willing to come to you should they see another employee breaking the standards and core beliefs.

In short, you need to act the same way you expect your employees to act. By contributing to certain core standards and values, your employees will follow suit. Furthermore, you'll find that the workplace will be friendlier as everyone knows what to expect from you and their co-workers. When you have a friendlier workplace, everyone will have higher morale which shows in how the employees work with each other and with customers.

Have the Ability to Delegate

One of the most important things you need to be able to do is trust your staff enough to delegate work. If you try to do it all yourself, especially once you pick up more customers, you'll spread yourself too thin and the quality of your work will suffer. You'll also find yourself producing less as you will dread coming in to face the pile of work. Dreading work leads to procrastination.

If you have a large company, you may want to delegate certain tasks to a specific department, but if you are a small company, you can delegate one or more tasks to an individual or a small group of individuals.

The ability to delegate tasks is an important skill. It doesn't work if you ask any one person to complete a certain task. You need to be able to choose the right person for a specific task so that the task is done properly and to your specifications.

Delegation doesn't work with just picking a person – be sure the person enjoys the task. You may have three people that have the ability to respond to customer service emails but only one person who enjoys answering emails all day. You'd do better picking the person that enjoys the task, as he or she will look forward to working every day and put more effort into the task.

Choosing staff members or employees to help with specific tasks also shows them that you trust them enough to give them the responsibility. This is great for employee morale. Furthermore, it gives you more time to attend to tasks that absolutely cannot be delegated to employees, such as payroll and other confidential jobs.

Summary

In closing, it might seem like you have to be Superman to be a good leader. After all, this is quite a list. But that is not so – if you stop and take a look at yourself, you may find that you already have many of these qualities.

If you don't have them all, create a list for yourself to refer to when you are not sure of something. Eventually, these leadership qualities will become second hand. If you still have problems creating the perfect office environment and getting people to follow your lead, have a powwow with some of your advisors. They will be able to give you more tips to help you accomplish what you need.

If you treat your employees and staff fairly and let them know you have an open door policy, you will find that the rest of the leadership qualities are easier to achieve.

Chapter 2
How to Present an Idea

Presenting an idea to an investor can be tricky business. If you don't present the idea in a fashion the investor likes, he or she will decline the resources required to get your idea in the works. One of the best things you can do is to get to know the investor, preferably on a more personal level. As you present more ideas, you gain experience even if the investor declines funding and resources. You don't have to start from a blank sheet – you can use some of these insights from an experienced view.

Know Your Audience

Before you present your idea, do a little research. You should be able to answer several questions before you meet with the investor.

- Who are the investors you plan to meet with? Do they represent a bank? Are they private investors? Banks are often stricter with regulations than private investors, thus it is harder to get financing. On the other hand, if you can present your idea in such a way that a bank will get you the resources you need, you will have a better interest rate. Private investors have more leeway in many areas including the amount they can fund. Certain banks may not fund over or under a certain amount. For example, Bank

A may not fund anything over $500,000 while Bank B may not fund a venture that is under $5,000,000.

- o Knowing your investors will also change how you present your idea, as well as the type of idea you are presenting. You need to consider many things in your presentation, including how you dress and your tone when you present your idea.

- o You must also take into consideration the type of investor you are working with – a private investor that never wears a suit or a banker who dresses in a three-piece suit every day will react in a different manner to the way you present yourself and your idea. You might present yourself a bit more laid back with a jeans-type guy than you would to someone who represents a major bank.

- o Regardless of whether your idea is for a white collar venture, a blue collar venture or a non-profit such as an animal rescue, your delivery must be professional and you must be prepared to answer questions about the venture, additional funding that may not be provided by the investor and several questions about the venture itself.

- o For example, if you want to start a wildlife sanctuary, you must know what special licenses and training you need to keep wildlife. You must also know that your employees and/or volunteers must obtain certain licenses just to enter certain enclosures.

- What do the investors care about? Part of the research you do on potential investors is finding out what personal interests the investor has. If your venture is a non-profit animal shelter, does the investor feel strongly about animal rescues? Has the investor provided resources for other animal shelters? Does the investor prefer wildlife shelters or dog rescue shelters? If the investor prefers dog rescue shelters, does he or she have emotional ties to a certain breed?

- o If you can answer these questions, you will know how to slant the interview so the investor sees you in a favorable light. Furthermore, if you have several investors to choose from, you will know who you should approach as a sponsor or coach, who to approach for financing, and who you should not approach with this particular venture. If you do not choose a certain investor this time, do not circular file his or her contact information. You may have another venture later that would be a perfect fit.

Know the Needs of the Business

Create a list of your business needs, ensuring that you provide a detailed explanation of the problem your venture solves. When crafting this discussion, be sure to craft it in such a way that shows the issues that must be rectified. Using the dog rescue venture as an example, there are many states with a high kill rate for certain breeds of dogs and dogs with certain issues. In many cases, the dogs are perfectly fine once they have some behavioral training and do not need to be put down. You may open a no-kill shelter for pit bulls. The shelter may need training specialists to properly train these dogs for behavior issues that manifested because of prior treatment.

The shelter may also need medical professionals to take care of animals that require medical care, which can be quite expensive in some cases. In some cases, a dog with medical issues may come into the shelter. If the dog's medical issues can be taken care of and its behavioral issues can be cured, the shelter could find the dog a forever home.

When you present this idea, you could approach it from the emotional standpoint that a dog should not be put down because it has food aggression and needs allergy treatment since both problems can be cured. You may also want to present some statistics to show how many dogs are needlessly put down every year.

Presenting Your Idea

Once you show the need, you need to present your idea in a distinct manner. Keeping it simple is best, so that the investor remembers the idea. You can use a metaphor to help the investor remember your idea. In the case of an animal shelter, you may tell the investor your venture keeps animals out of the lion's den – a kill shelter – and rehabilitates them so they can live a full, happy life with a family that is willing to treat the animal well, including continuing behavioral training and medical care.

Some dogs that were going to be put down due to aggression issues have earned their Canine Good Citizen awards and are now therapy dogs. Depending on how far you want to take the animal rescue venture, your final goal could be to rehabilitate problem dogs to become therapy dogs, search dogs, police dogs or dogs used in the medical community as cancer sniffers or therapy dogs for children instead of just making sure the dogs go to a good family home.

Outline Your Audience

You must have an audience or your venture will fail. Without customers or clients, you have no income, thus knowing your audience is an important part of showing need for resources. It shows the investor that you care about your venture and that others are interested and will benefit from your venture, thus they will support your venture.

Using the animal shelter example, your audience is those who would like a dog, whether as a companion or a therapy dog. Some people prefer a rescue dog over a dog from a breeder. You can give research examples of the success of competitors, but if your idea is something brand new, there won't be much research.

In this case, you might talk about alternatives your venture offers to people and why your idea is different and why the market will support it. In the case of the animal shelter, "throw away" dogs now become dogs that are needed for a specific purpose, whether sniffing out corpses – or those still alive, but injured -- in a building collapse, finding a lost child, helping a disabled person with day-to-day tasks or even putting a smile on a hospital-bound child's face.

Your sustainable competitive advantage in this example would be that you are training dogs to be helpful to society and can command a higher adoption fee because of the training put into these dogs.

What's in it for the Investor?

You have to figure out why the investor would want to invest in your venture. It could be an emotional reason, it could be because the money the investor will make will fairly compensate him or her for the resources, or it could be a combination of both.

If you can meet with the investor in an informal setting prior to presenting your idea, you can get a better idea of what makes him or her tick. If you find the investor doesn't care for animals and you're opening a shelter or rescue, it's probably a good idea to present this idea to another investor. This doesn't mean that you have to give up on this investor, but you may have a better chance with someone who loves animals.

What's in it for You?

The investor will also want to know how much you care about your idea. He or she will look to see how much of your own resources you invest in your idea. The investor will also look to see whether others have or will invest in your idea. He or she will also see how emotional you are about your venture. A person that is emotionally tied to a venture has a better chance of succeeding.

When you approach the investor, you should have a table showing how much you invested and where you plan on getting additional resources. For example, if you need $100,000 so that you can add another building to your animal rescue facility, plus you need funds to pay an on-site veterinarian and trainer, you might show that you have $20,000 to put into the building; and that the veterinarian and trainer are willing to work for a lower fee than they would have charged if they worked for another facility.

If you show that you are also willing to invest in your own idea, the investor will be more likely to help you out. Your own investment shows that you care about the idea enough to do everything possible to make it work; and that you and others are willing to take some of the risk.

Since the investor is also looking for commitment, not just how much money you have invested, showing that you actually work to implement and continue carrying out your idea also encourages him or her to help you get your idea off the ground. You may hold a pertinent position within the company or you may even be on site to supervise the entire operation – just as long as you are not an absentee owner.

Describe Your Team

After careful planning, your team is the most important part of making your idea succeed. The investor will also look at your team of people to see how they are vested in your idea. If you have people who believe in you and your idea, they are more likely to help ensure your success.

Your animal trainer is a big part of your success, especially if you are training dogs to be service animals. Without a trainer, your business would fail. Thus, when presenting your idea to an investor, discuss your employees. Tell him or her of the trainer's experience and give some examples of what the trainer has achieved.

The people who work in the front office – those who interact directly with customers – are also important. These people must not only be friendly and customer service oriented, but (in a rescue or shelter setting) must love animals and cannot be intimidated by problem animals.

All businesses have certain risks – you may also discuss how employees' backgrounds and experiences cover certain risks.

Let's Talk About Money

This is the part you have to carefully research -- if you ask for too much money; you may not get what you need, however, if you ask for too little, you won't be able to successfully implement your idea.

Figuring what you need for material items is the easy part. If you are building an addition, you can get a quote from a builder. But you may have other things you need financing for, such as hiring a professional. If you can find a professional willing to wait a few weeks or months for you to implement your idea, you can agree upon a yearly paycheck, thus making it easier to get the resources to facilitate that part of the idea.

If you have to wait to hire a professional because it will take six months to construct the additional space, you may have to create a budget for a professional. In this case, it is best to speak to several in the field to learn the average yearly salary. You can also use federal web sites to check the average local salary for the professional.

When planning the figure you need to request, be sure to include the small things. Depending on your idea, you may need computers, medical supplies, office supplies and furniture to get started. If the "small" things are things you can get without resources, write them down anyway – this shows the investor that you thought of everything; plus it shows that you are also investing in your idea.

Keep in mind that the term "small" is relative. You may be investing in $30,000 in office furniture and computers, but in the realm of things, this is small potatoes compared to what you need to make your idea jump.

Measuring Success

Your investors will want to know if you succeeded in implementing and following through with your idea. At any rate, you should be keeping records for expenses, profits and other financial records.

In addition to financial records, you should also show that your business is successfully implementing the program. In the case of the animal shelter, you may show the investors financials, but you should also show the dogs that have been rehomed or that have been successful in getting a new job with the police department, a search and rescue facility or with a person that does hospital therapy. Depending on the type of venture you have, a picture could say a thousand words.

If you have a goal that will take several months or longer to implement, you may want to create a pilot of your service to show the investors how the idea will work. The pilot should also show success points. For example, you may expect to complete 1,000 service calls during the first six months or sell 10,000 units in the first six months. The pilot will allow investors to see how you are going to measure success over a long term project.

Prototypes

You may also create a prototype of your idea. Whether it is a product or a large project that involves additional real estate, you can build a mock up to show the investor what the project will look like. In the case of additional real estate, including buildings, if it is too expensive to build a 3D sample, you can create a 2D drawing or sketch to show the investor what the finished product should look like.

Summary

Before you approach investors, it is best to be prepared with as much information as possible. You obviously need information about your idea, including the length of time it will take to implement the idea, but you also need information about the investors you are going to approach.

Create a prototype if funds allow, and if not, at least a drawing of your idea. You should also have a timeline of goals to reach. If the investor wishes to receive updates as to whether you are achieving your goals, be prepared to show them via reports and pictures.

Chapter 3
Bringing Your Product to Market

You've come up with a good idea for something no one else made; but there are many things you need to do before you sell your product to people. You could just make the product, but you would waste a lot of money in making and selling it if someone else stole your idea. You can patent your idea – this means you register it with the U.S. Patent and Trademark Office. Then, if someone tries to steal your idea, you can take that person or company to court because you have proof it was your idea. Before you even register it, which costs money, you need to make sure that your idea has not been thought of by someone else and if not, that people will actually use it.

Where Do You Find Ideas?

You could probably sit and think for days and months to try to come up with an idea that hasn't been thought of already; and you would be wasting a lot of time unless you could come up with something. Usually, when someone has a great idea for something that the rest of the world could use it is because that person needed a special tool or wanted a computer to do something specific. For example, a mechanic would find use for a lighted socket.

A socket is used to remove nuts and bolts. It could be long or short and comes in many different sizes. Sometimes you have to reach a bolt way in the back of the engine and it's too dark to see. You could try hanging a light on the hood of the car, but because of the shape of the engine, the light doesn't shine where you need it. A socket with a light in it will help you find the bolt you need to take out. Someone got frustrated because it was taking too much time to get the bolt out since he couldn't see it. He got the bright idea of making a socket with a light in it. Before he could sell his product, he had to do a lot of work to get it to market.

Before you can even start designing the product, you have to find out if your idea is something a lot of people would use.

Is Your Idea Something Many People Would Use?

If your idea is something many people will use, you will be able to sell enough to pay for the cost of making the product plus make some money for yourself. In the case of the lighted socket, the person who invented it knew that mechanics often had problems seeing nuts and bolts behind the engine or under the engine where it is dark. He did his research and learned that a lot of mechanics would like a lighted socket so they could fix cars faster and to make the job easier.

You have more of a chance to succeed if you do research about the market before you start planning your project and before you spend the money to patent the idea. Finding out whether people would use your product is part of a study you need to do before you start spending money on your idea.

Turning Your Idea into a Product

You have to do a lot of research – a feasibility study – to make sure people will use the product and that the product will actually work. When you do a feasibility study, you have to write down all the information about your product, who will buy it, and you have to make sure that someone else didn't register the same idea with the U.S. Patent and Trademark Office.

If your product is just a little different from something that is already for sale, then you have to come up with a new idea. It makes no sense to pay to create something that already exists.

Once you find that your idea does not already exist, you need to plan who is going to manufacture your product. This means you need to know how much money you need to get started. This is called the "startup cost."

Part of the startup cost is determining how you will get customers. This is called "customer acquisition." Most advertising is not free, so there will be a cost to reach out to potential customers.

Startup costs also include marketing to the people you found to buy your product, money for attorneys to draft contracts and agreements between you and the people you may be working with to create your product, and money to purchase land, buildings, equipment and to pay employees.

The Market

If your product is similar enough to someone else's product, you may have a lot of competition. Competition means that someone else is selling the same thing you are selling; and people could decide to buy someone's product instead of yours. If your product is something that hasn't been invented yet or is something that is different enough from anything else already for sale, then you don't have a lot of competition. This means that it is a little easier to find new customers.

For example, if you have 1,000 people or companies who say they need your product and no one else makes something like you have, you could have 1,000 sales. If someone in your city sells something that is almost like your product, you might only sell to 500 people or companies instead of 1,000. Because your product is new, you will most likely sell less since other people are already selling something that is almost the same. People know the other company's product works, but they don't know if yours works because it is new.

You have to prove your product is as good -- or -- better than the other company's or person's product. This is something that you should keep in mind when you are designing your product. You might buy a competitor's product to see what materials are used to make it and how it works. If you can use better materials or give the product another feature, then you have a better chance of beating the competition.

In the lighted socket example, if the other person's uses small watch batteries to power an incandescent light bulb, you may want to use more batteries or larger batteries to power an LED light, which uses less energy. This means that the customer will spend less money on batteries, so you have a "one up" on the competition.

Figuring Out Who You Should Ask to Buy Your Product

Before you can determine how long it will take you to get customers, you have to figure out who are the people most likely to buy your product. This is called "targeting." If your invention is the socket with a light, you might target men in the 18 to 55 age bracket. These are the people most likely working as mechanics; and mechanics are the people most likely to buy this invention.

Keep in mind that people who are younger or older may buy your invention; and women are sometimes mechanics or work on their own cars, too, so they may buy your invention. But, your biggest group of buyers will be men from 18 to 55 years of age.

Once you know who will most likely buy and use your invention, you should add to your research by reading newsletters, magazines and blogs about mechanics. You might also attend trade shows to start making contacts.

Once you learn about the market – the people who would use your invention – you can determine who would most likely purchase your product.

Research Your Market

When you start to research your market, there are three questions you should answer. The questions all center on future customers – this is your market.

- Who are your customers? You already did part of the work in figuring out who your customers are by knowing what age and sex would most likely buy your product. Now you have to add to that information. You need to know what income bracket would most likely buy your product. To do this, you need to know how much it costs to produce the product.

  o In addition, if someone else is selling something similar, you can't price yourself out of the market. Another piece of information you need to gather is how much other people are selling products that are similar to yours. If your product has better quality, you may be able to ask a higher price, but if it's too high, people won't buy it no matter how good it is.

- The next thing you need to ask yourself is how you reach those customers. Some people respond to phone calls, some respond to direct mail and some prefer digital advertising, like email or social media. You can find out what people prefer by contacting them to ask them if they are interested in your product and how you should contact them when the product is ready for sale.

- If you are selling to a retailer, you also need to know how many the store will buy from you and when they expect the product to be ready. Many stores will buy things that are in season – this means that if you are selling a piece of wool clothing, they may only buy it in the late summer. But, if you have a product that could be used no matter what the season – such as a lighted socket – then the time to sell isn't as important.

You definitely don't want to approach a store that doesn't sell tools if your idea is a lighted socket. You would be wasting your time and the store's time because they don't sell items like that. You do want to approach stores that sell only tools or tools and other items. Even stores that sell only car parts may be interested in buying something like a special lighted socket.

How to Get Customers Interested in Your Product

You can either make a few samples of your product or you can make a brochure with all of the information about the product. It is better to do both. If you can find a factory to make several samples, you can give a sample to each store, plus you can hand out a brochure that tells the store why the product is a good idea, why their customers will buy it and why the store should sell it.

Before you can make samples, you need to make a prototype. The prototype doesn't have to be made of the same material that the finished product will be made from, but it must work. This part of the process of bringing a product to market is the first expensive part of the process. The expense depends on many things, including whether the invention has a lot of moving parts, takes a long time to program if you invented a special computer program, or is made from expensive materials.

The prototype also helps with filing the patent on your invention. You can use it to help fill out the application documents. If you use an attorney to complete the patent process – and you should – the attorney will have the prototype in his hands while he completes the patent process. This gives those helping you a better idea of how your product is supposed to work and what it looks like.

If money is a factor, you can also create a virtual prototype. This is a three-dimensional computer model of your invention. The virtual prototype is visible on all different angles. If the invention has moving parts, you can even create an animated prototype to show what your invention looks like and how it moves.

Applying for a Patent

Before you put out any money into creating and researching your invention, you should have done a patent search. The patent search tells you if someone else has already invented the same thing you are trying to create and sell. Since you already know that no one has created the same invention you did, you can patent your invention so no one else can create it and make money from it.

When applying for a patent, you should hire an attorney to help you. There are several different strategies you can use for your patent application. Depending on the type of invention you are creating, these might include trade secrets, a utility patent, a design patent, a provisional patent or you may want to have a longer patent pending strategy.

You may use trade secrets if you are creating a special computer program. If it is going to take a while to create your invention and get it out to enough people, you may want to have the patent pending for a longer time. Because patents do expire after a certain number of years, you may also want to speak to your attorney about a longer patent pending strategy. You can also use a patent to keep others from using a company name or logo.

Picking the Right Business Model

You can choose one of three ways to produce your invention. Of course, starting a company is the most expensive, but it could be the highest money maker for you.

- Outsourcing: You can hire a company to make your invention. You research different factories to find which one would produce the best product for you. Things you might look at is whether the factory can produce the number of units you need, whether they can meet deadlines, quality of their materials and the quality of the finished product. This is the lowest risk to you and is an excellent option for an inventor who does not have a lot of money.

- Licensing: In this case, you sell your idea to a company and the company pays you a little bit – a royalty – for each sale. You don't earn as much money as you would if you hired a company to make your product or if you were to start a new company, but your responsibility ends when you sell the idea.

- Starting Your Own Company: If you can get the money to start your own company, this is the best option. You have to have enough money to buy land, the building, the machines, pay employees and pay bills among other things. This is the option with the biggest risk but allows you to make the most money since you control where you get the materials used to produce your invention.

Get Ready to Rumble!

Once you decide which type of business model you want to go with, you need to close the deal. In all three cases, you will need an attorney to help you draft the legal documents required to seal the deal.

If you are outsourcing, you should choose at least three different factories, then tour the factories. While the factory owners may tell you one thing over the phone, you should tour the factory to make sure the factory does what the owner says it will do – after all, these people want your business. In addition to checking things like quality of materials, you need to check several other things such as the factory's licensing, its safety record, how it treats its employees and, most importantly, the factory's financials. After all, you don't want a factory that is in debt as they could close and leave you in a lurch.

If you are starting your own company, you will need to buy the land and building. If you buy an existing building on land, you may have to renovate the building. You will attend a closing where you take title to the land, sign the mortgage if you don't buy it with cash, and get the keys. Then you can start renovations.

If you are buying land only, then you have to find a builder to build the factory. At this point, you should hire an architect to draw the building plans. Once you have the building plans, then you need to find a builder you like to build the factory for you. Once that has been completed, you need to find the equipment to make your product. After you get the equipment installed and the offices set up, then you can start hiring employees.

While you are looking at employees' resumes, you should be making sure that you have all the licenses required by your city, county and state to run the factory. You should also make sure that you have enough of the right kind of insurance for your company.

In addition to insurance, you will need to pay worker's compensation insurance. It is a good idea to have the best insurance you can afford because people tend to get hurt in factories, even when they are careful. Don't forget, they are working with large machines.

If you are selling your idea, your attorney will help you draft the documents you need to ensure that you get paid for the royalties on every unit you sell. Once you are happy with the documents, your attorney will give them to the person or company you chose to buy your invention. If the person or company agrees, then you give up your idea. The documents should have an initial amount for the idea, plus a pay schedule and amount for each unit sold so you know about how much you will be getting and when you should expect a check.

Using a Business Plan

You have a lot of decisions to make once you come up with an idea that you think others will buy from you. Once you come up with the idea, you have a lot of legal work to do in addition to getting the prototype done, the patent filed and the samples done so that you can approach businesses or individuals to sell your invention.

No matter which method you choose, you should create a business plan. Chances are you'll have to borrow money to turn your idea into a useful product. The business plan will tell banks, investors and partners how you plan on creating your product and how you plan to present it to customers. It also shows which customers you will most likely approach.

The business plan will also help you decide whether you want to hire a factory, sell your idea to someone else or start your own business. When you have everything planned out banks and investors are more willing to lend you the money to get your idea out to the public.

The business plan also keeps you on track. You may have everything planned out in your head, but it is really easy to make a huge mistake by skipping a step in the process. Even the smallest step is important to the success of your invention. A business plan doesn't allow you to skip anything and you have more chances to succeed.

Summary

In a nutshell, once you come up with an idea, you have to create a prototype, find customers to buy your product and decide whether you are going to outsource to another factory, sell your idea or start your own company.

Each method has several hurdles you need to jump to make your invention successful. Even though you have a business plan, you may want to make smaller lists for each section of the business plan. As you go through the steps, you can cross them off the smaller "to do" lists.

When you get to the point where you have to choose an attorney to help you with the legal documents, be sure to choose someone who does extensive business law. A lawyer who drafts bad contracts could cost you success.

If you follow your business plan and put your best foot forward during all stages of bringing your product to market, you have a much better chance of succeeding.

Chapter 4
What is a Bank and What Does it Do?

If you have $1,000 that you don't need right away, but you want to earn more money – interest – on that $1,000, you deposit the money in the bank. The bank pays you to hold your money. When you put money in the bank, it is called a deposit. When the bank pays you to hold your money, it is called "interest."

The bank also lends money, and when it does, it collects interest. If you want to buy a go-cart that costs $500 but you don't have that much, you can ask the bank to lend you the money. If you have a way to pay the bank back, the bank will lend you the money and it will charge you interest.

This is how banks make money and can afford to pay you interest on your deposit. The interest the bank pays you is less than the interest it collects from the person who borrowed money. This means that if you deposit $1,000 and the bank pays you 5 percent interest, which is $50 dollars per month, every month your balance – the amount you have in your bank account – goes up. After the first month, you will have $1,050 in the bank. After the second month, you will have $1,102.50.

Now, if another person borrows $500, the bank might charge that person 10 percent per month. This means that the person who borrowed the money has to pay back the $500 plus $50 the first month. If the payment on the $500 is only $25, the next month the person who borrowed the money will owe $475 plus 10 percent interest, which means his payment would be $72.50: $25 plus 10 percent of $475. The bank is making a lot of money so has some to pay you interest on your deposit, plus some extra, which is called "profit."

The bank uses profits to pay the people who work there, the rent on the bank building and to pay for electricity, telephones and other bills.

Where Does My Money Go?

When you make a deposit, the bank teller puts the money with everyone else's money. The teller enters the amount you gave him into the computer to keep track of how much of that money belongs to you. This is called your balance. Your balance goes up when you add more money and goes down when you take money out of the bank. The bank uses everyone's money to make loans to people who want to borrow money.

Why Do People Borrow Money from the Bank?

In most cases, people can't borrow money from their parents or from friends or even a stranger because those people might not have that much money. Plus, how would those people know they would get their money back? That is part of what banks do – they hold your money and they lend money to people who want to buy something that costs a lot. It is also how the bank makes money to pay the people who work there.

How Else Do Banks Make Money?

Not everyone needs to borrow money all the time; and not everyone can afford to borrow money. If a person does not go to work every day, the bank will not let that person borrow money because he has no way to pay it back. When banks do lend money, it takes a long time to get the money back because people pay it back a little at a time – in payments. Because of this the bank has to have another way to make money. Banks charge the people who deposit money a bank fee to use the bank's services. If you have a checking account – a place to store your money until you need it to pay bills – the bank might charge you a little bit every month to help pay the bank's bills. This is called a bank fee.

Who Can Deposit Money in the Bank?

Any person or company that has a bank account can deposit money in the bank. Big companies deposit lots of money when they sell things. When you go to the fair and have to pay money to get in, the people at the fair deposit the money in their bank. That money is used to pay people who work at the fair and for the electricity the fair needs to make the rides work. It is also used to buy some of the ingredients needed to make that wonderful cotton candy and funnel cakes that you can buy at the fair.

Since a lot of people go to the fair, the fair collects a lot of money. To keep the money safe and to make it easier to pay people to keep the fair running, all that money is deposited in the bank. This is also how banks can lend money to people who need it – because big companies and people with a lot of money keep their money in the bank.

What is Better: A Checking or Savings Account?

This depends on how you want to use the money. If you have bills to pay every month, it is better to have a checking account because your money is always there for you to use. If you don't need your money for a long time, you might decide to put it in a savings account. Some banks tell you that if you put your money in a savings account, you can't use it for some time. Sometimes that might be for a few months, or it could be a year or longer.

Even though you cannot use that money right away, it is earning you extra money. Because the bank is holding your money and lending it to other people, it must pay you. The bank pays you in the form of interest.

More About Making Loans?

You may be thinking that you might need your money and are wondering how you will get it if the bank lent it to someone else. Most of the time, a person who deposits money into a savings account does not need his money right away. Because of this, banks can use deposits from a lot of people – these are called short-term deposits because the bank knows that you will eventually need your money – to make long-term loans.

It takes people longer to pay the bank back, but during that time, other people keep making deposits. Plus – don't forget – the bank makes money on fees that it charges for people to use the bank to store money; and it makes money on interest that it charges people to borrow money. This process is called maturity transformation. When a bank makes a loan, it is called an asset because the person who borrowed the money has to pay it back.

Most of the money the bank makes comes from interest it collects on the money it loaned to other people. Another way banks make money is to give or issue securities. These are usually commercial paper or bonds. The bank owns these securities and can lend them out to other banks in exchange for cash money. The bank uses the cash money to pay you for your deposit and to pay other things like bills and the people who work at the bank.

When a bank does this, it must pay interest to the bank who lent them the cash. The other bank makes money. Securities are another form of savings. When a bank trades cash money for another bank's securities, it also makes money on the loan. These types of "trades" or transactions are called "repurchase agreements."

A bank can also sell their loans. This is often referred to as "selling paper." When a bank makes a loan for a house, the person who borrowed the money has to sign a mortgage. This is an agreement between the person who borrowed the money and the bank; and it shows that the person who borrowed the money has to pay it back to the bank.

The bank takes many mortgages and adds them together. If 50 different people borrowed $100,000 to buy houses that means that the bank is owed $5,000,000. This is another asset – something the bank owns. The money is not in the bank's vault, but in an agreement stating that each person owes the bank.

The bank can bundle the mortgages together and sell them at a discount rate to another bank so it can have most of the cash back right away. The bank might sell $5,000,000 in mortgages to another bank for $4,000,000. The bank who bought the mortgages pays the bank who is selling them $4,000,000. The bank that paid the cash collects the money from the people who borrowed the money. If everyone pays their mortgage, the new bank will make $1,000,000 plus the interest.

The bank that got the cash in exchange for the mortgages can use the money to lend to other people. The bank will charge an interest rate high enough to make the $1,000,000 it lost by selling the mortgages at a discount, plus a little more profit. This process is called "liquidity transformation and securitization."

Bank Transactions

Banks not only allow you to save and borrow money, but they also create money with a "domestic and international payments system." If you deposit money into a checking account, you have to be able to use that money to pay other people. You may want to buy groceries, pay the light bill or you may need to make a house payment. Another part of this is when you work, you get paid for the work you do for someone.

The banks process the payments needed for people to live life. Your boss puts money into the bank when he sells something. He has to pay you for working for him, so he transfers some of that money to you. He can do that by writing you a check or by transferring the money by way of an electronic transaction. A check is a piece of paper that says someone owes you money. When you take the check to the bank, the bank subtracts the amount from your boss's account and adds it to your account.

You can pay your bills the same way. After you earn money and your boss gives you a check or makes an electronic deposit to your account, you can use the money to pay your bills or to buy groceries. You can write a check or pay by debit card. You can even go to the bank and take money out and give cash to the grocery store when you buy groceries. If you were to write a check for groceries, the grocery store would deposit the check. The store's bank adds money to the store's bank account and subtracts it from your bank account.

If something were to happen to the payment system, people could not pay bills. If your boss cannot pay you because the bank's payment system is not working properly, then you won't be able to buy groceries. The ability to buy goods and services is called trade. If the payment system is not working, people cannot trade things for money and the economic growth – the amount people in general spend – does not grow as fast. This means that everyone suffers because there may be shortages on food, gas and other things that people need to live.

Other Ways Banks Can Create Money

Banks are not allowed to lend out all the money people deposit. They must keep some; and this is called "reserves." The bank can hold reserves in the form of cash money or securities – securities can be easily converted to cash money. The bank figures out how much money people take out of their savings and checking accounts.

It also has rules it has to follow. A "central bank," or in the case of banks in the United States, the Federal Reserve Bank, tells banks how much money they have to keep in the bank. This means that if you deposit $1,000, the bank cannot use all of your money – it can only use some of your money so that it has money ready to give you when you are ready to take your money out to buy something.

A bank can also sell insurance and mutual funds to raise money. Another thing that is tied into mortgages is loan servicing. A bank can charge a person who borrows money to take care of the loan. This is called loan servicing. In this process, the bank collects money from the person who borrowed money and adjusts the borrower's balance when the borrower pays every month.

A bank can agree with another bank or company to service their loans. If this is the case, the bank collects the payments from people who borrowed money, then sends the money to the other bank or company. The bank that is collecting the money charges the other bank or company a fee to collect money.

Transmitting Monetary Policy

When the economy grows, everyone makes money. This could – in some circumstances -- cause inflation. Inflation is the amount prices rise compared against the amount of money people make (purchasing power). If inflation goes up 2 percent, that means that the candy you paid $1 for today will cost $1.02 next year.

Banks control all of the money. The central bank controls the money throughout the nation, but local banks can also control money. The central bank can change the rules and tell your bank how much money it has to keep in reserves. If the amount is higher than it was before the central bank changed the rules, that means the local bank has less money to lend.

When a bank has less money to lend, it charges more interest to people who want to borrow the money. A local bank can also decide to put more of its deposits into the reserves. If the central bank or a local bank decides to put too much money in reserves and there is less money to loan people, the nation suffers a "credit crunch." That is because there isn't enough money to lend. This is when the cost of borrowing money goes up.

If people can't borrow money then they can't buy expensive things like new cars and houses. If your neighbor lost his job and can't pay for his house, he would have to sell his house. But if the banks are not lending money, he won't be able to sell the house because no one will be able to get the loan to buy the house.

This means that the neighbor can't sell his house and he can't make the house payment, so the bank takes the house. Now the bank has a house that it can't move into – because banks don't set up shop in houses – and no cash because the person who borrowed the money can't buy it back and because another person can't buy it since the banks don't have the money to lend to other people. This is one of the most common ways to hurt the economy.

When the economy fails, banks can also fail. If people who deposit money in the bank no longer trust the bank, they will take all of their money out of the bank. Since the bank lends out some of the money, it can't afford to pay every person his money. This is how a bank fails. The FDIC insures the people's money in the event that something like this happens, but it only insures $100,000. If you have $200,000 in the same bank, you will only get $100,000 of that money if the bank fails before you can get your money out.

Banks can also fail because it has more checking accounts than other sources of income and because it doesn't have a lot of cash, but has a lot of assets. Not all assets can be turned into cash (sold) right away. This means a bank could be rich because of the assets it owns, but it doesn't have any cash money to give to people who hold accounts at the bank.

Bank Regulation

The rules that banks must follow are designed to keep banks from failing – in most cases. If a bank fails, people tend to panic and withdraw their money, causing a bad situation to become worse.

A bank can take an emergency loan from the central bank if it has to so that it doesn't fail. Most countries also require a bank to have a charter. A charter is how a bank is formed and it contains the rules that the bank must follow. A bank must also insure its deposits up to a certain amount. In the United States, that amount is $100,000 per bank account.

If a bank does business in another country, they must also follow that country's banking rules. The rules also state that banks cannot do certain things as far as credit and the market go. A bank cannot invest in companies or people with bad credit – people who don't pay their bills. A bank must also keep more of their profits just like you would keep your money in a savings account.

If the bank is going to fail, then it has some savings to help it survive until it gets back on its feet. This is called "capital." Banks that operate in many countries have to have more capital than local banks. A bank must also keep a certain amount of liquid assets such as securities. Liquid assets are those that can be sold immediately for cash.

Summary

If you want to save up for something special, you can open a bank account with your parents. This is a good way to learn how to save money early and how to manage a bank account. Ask your parents to help you open a savings account that pays interest. Put part of your allowance in the bank account. Once you get older and start babysitting or mowing lawns, you can add some of that money to the bank account.

Chapter 5
How to Write a Press Release

A press release is one of the best public relations strategies a company can use to get exposure. You can use a press release to announce an event, a product release, new management, a merger or an acquisition among other newsworthy events. This short document should grab a journalist's interest enough to entice him or her to further cover the topic. It's a great way to get free exposure to millions of viewers, readers or listeners, which means thousands – at the very least – of potential customers.

When crafting a press release, you must make it stand out like a sore thumb because journalists see tons of pitches and potential stories every day. The press release format is basic, but the content should be different and riveting, and at the same time, professional. There are eight steps to writing a press release that grabs the reader by the shirt collar and says, "Hey! Pick me!"

Create a Great Headline

The headline, like the title of a book or great magazine article, is the first thing the reader sees. If the headline doesn't grab the reader's attention, your press release is going to end up in the circular file. The headline is the first thing a reader reads, but it is the last thing that should be written, as you can then choose the most important idea.

Not only should the headline grab the reader's attention, but it should use sales psychology while being very specific. With a specific headline, you are able to communicate the subject of your press release instantly, and show that the content is interesting and new.

Don't use the first headline you come up with – write several, and then pick the best three. You can combine the best parts of each headline and simplify it so that it is short 'n sweet. The headline should make the reader curious, grab his or her emotions and make the reader feast his or her eyes on the rest of the copy.

An excellent headline also uses sales psychology by luring the reader to move past the headline. Don't let the reader give a negative answer to the inherent question contained in the headline. Sales psychology arouses a reader's curiosity and doesn't allow him or her to walk away without reading more.

For example, instead of asking if a person wants Option A or Option B, which could elicit a negative response, ask which option the person wants. While the person could say "neither," the first thing that enters his or her head is, "I need to choose one." Apply this thought process to the headline to encourage the reader to put the press release in the "I need to read this" pile instead of the circular file.

Get to the Point

Don't drag your readers through the entire document without giving them something to latch onto. They'll get bored with it if you don't get to the point right away, then all the work you put into a great headline goes down the drain.

Journalists are busy, so if a headline catches their attention, they will start reading and may only get to the first few sentences, or they may actually read the first sentence and scan the rest of the press release. Thus, you need to get your message to the reader and convince him or her to immediately read further.

If the press release has more than one important point, make sure you reach all of them in the first few sentences.

Additional paragraphs are for supporting information. You might expound on statistics or in the case of an event, discuss the location and happenings at the event. If you are holding a fund raiser and a popular singer is slated to appear, be sure you mention that person or group in the headline, then in later paragraphs for additional information.

Include Statistics and Hard Numbers

When you support the significance of your announcement with hard numbers, you create compelling content. This is especially important if you're claiming a trend such as the popularity of a certain designer or a statistic for a city.

For example, if a criminal defense attorney states that his city has one of the highest murder rates, he or she may find the murder rate plus other rate breakdowns such as murder in the commission of burglary or murder during a domestic violence dispute for his or her city. Often, governmental web sites – federal, state and local – may have this information. Colleges and other groups that conduct studies may have statistics listed on their web sites.

An example for a fundraiser event with a popular singer would be to introduce a popular singer and mention that the person won awards or sells out every concert. Provide the number of awards and attendance numbers, e.g., five Grammys and sell-out crowds averaging 60,000 people.

Perfection Rules

Proofreading is an important part of creating the perfect press release. Once you write it, proofread it carefully. Let it go until the next morning then proofread it again. Because it is very difficult to catch your own mistakes, have two or three friends or co-workers proofread the press release. Be sure to tell them to be harsh in their criticism as some friends might tell you that it looks great instead of being honest.

Just one mistake can make a reader discard your press release as he or she will not take you seriously. Press releases must be professional, which means perfect spelling and grammar.

Another tip for proofreading is to convert the text to another format. You can convert a Word document to Adobe or you can increase the font in the Word document. Doing this often makes mistakes stand out because of the different format or text size.

Including Quotations

A quote from someone in the company or from someone involved with manufacturing the product or setting up the event can add flavor to the press release. A quote also provides additional information about the product, service or event.

You can ask an employee for a quote, or you may remember something catchy that someone said while discussing the topic contained in the press release. Be sure you ask the employee if you can use his or her name and the quote. If the press release does get published, that person's name and quote will be in front of a lot of people.

The quote could be something humorous or it could be a statistic from the manufacturer of a product. Regardless of what you choose, make sure it makes the product, service or event stand out.

Contact Information

Don't forget to include your contact information in the press release. Without it, the press release is ineffective. If a journalist cannot get in touch with you to get more information, he or she will not publish an otherwise great press release. You should put your contact information at the top of the press release, and it should include, at a minimum, your phone number and email address.

Your contact information also allows a journalist to call you back at a later time to ask if you'd like to do a follow up article on the event. A follow up interview may include how much you money you collected in a fundraiser, how you changed a person's life because of certain services or even a donation of your retail sales to help someone down on his or her luck. This is more free advertising for your company or group.

If your press release is about your company going public you could create a follow up press release to tell people how well your stock sold on its first day; and if you are selling private stock, what your expansion plans are for the next year.

Keep it Short 'n Sweet

Limit the press release to one page if possible. If you have to use a second page, it is acceptable, but keep in mind that the shorter the press release, the better. This forces you to delete any information that is not important or that doesn't convey urgency. Because a journalist is usually limited on space, he or she looks for stories that are short and to the point.

To get the best information in the press release, write without any constrictions. Read through the document and delete any information that doesn't convey urgency and importance to the reader. This information can be presented on the web site or in additional documentation through email. When you are done, you should have a document that tells the reader the most important information about the event.

Providing Access to More Information

Though you should limit your press release to one or two pages, that doesn't mean you can't give people more information. Include links to your web site in the press release. Make sure the web site has more information that directly relates to the content in the press release. If the content is on a separate page on your web site, provide the direct link instead of making the reader go to the main page to search for the content.

You might include your mission, a few paragraphs about what you've previously accomplished and more information about the product, service or event.

If you do not have a web site, offer an email with additional information. Ask readers to send an email to you for more information. You can set up an auto-responder to send a document containing more information about the event or product.

If you are doing a follow up press release, create a new web page with the event statistics. If your press release was about raising money by selling stock, keep people apprised of your expansion progress. These are things to keep people coming back to your web site, thus in the front of their minds.

Examples of Great Headlines

A criminal defense attorney may use "New Report Identifies Cities with Highest Murder Rate" to let the world know he or she defends those accused of manslaughter or murder if his city is listed in the report.

A museum might use "Lost Works of [famous artist] Found in [city] Attic" to let people know it has a new exhibit with these works of art.

A retailer might announce beating a goal by using a headline that states, "[Retailer] Beats Goal of 10,000 Sales for Third Quarter." This headline will get people to read it simply because they want to know how many sales the retailer actually had.

An entity holding a fundraiser may use a celebrity's name in the headline: "Wildlife Sanctuary Fundraiser Features [celebrity name]." In this case, if the press release is also published online, it will garner the attention of those searching that celebrity's name. People who would not have searched for your fundraiser would see it.

Summary

Creating a great press release is not something you can do in a matter of minutes. It takes a great deal of thought and planning. To get to the meat of the whole document, start with rambling thoughts about the product or event. Write everything down, whether you do it in paragraph form or in list form. If you do work better with the paragraph form, be sure to keep each thought in its own paragraph.

Get other pertinent information you would like to see in the press release, including statistics and quotations. Once you have everything you need, find the most important aspects of what you need to convey. These should make up your first paragraph. One of the statistics should be in the first paragraph.

Everything else is considered additional information and needs to go into subsequent well-organized paragraphs.

Once you have completed the entire press release, create an attention-grabbing title that will keep the press release in front of the reader's eyeballs long enough to keep his or her interest. If it keeps the reader's interest, there is a good chance the journalist will choose your press release for publishing.

Chapter 6
How to Write a Business Plan

When you want to start a new business, there are many things that you must do before you can even get a store front or order inventory and hire employees. The business plan discusses all the plans needed to start the business, including how much money you think you will need, what part of the city you want to open your business and how much time it will take for you to pay a business loan back – if you take a loan.

If you take a loan, or even if you don't take a loan, then the business plan will show how long you expect to break even and how long it takes to make a profit. Breaking even means getting the money you spent to open the business back in the bank. Making a profit means that you earn enough money to pay all of the bills plus have extra for yourself to live on and enjoy life.

Why Do You Need a Business Plan?

A business plan helps you decide many things about your new business, including how much money you need to get started, how much money the business will make in the first year and how much money the business will make in the first five years. Why five years? Most business plans outline five years because the last two are the only profitable years. Some businesses will be successful during their first years, but it is rare. Five years give banks, investors and partners an idea of how you want to build the business.

- The initial startup cost is how much money you need to start the business and keep it running for a certain amount of time. Many people calculate initial startup costs for the first year. If you want to sell things such as toys at your business, you need to know how much it will cost to:

    o Register the business with the state and city. Each state and city – and sometimes the county you live in, makes you get special licenses to run the business. You will also need to check to see if you need any other special licenses. If you work with certain chemicals, you may have to get an additional license. Good examples of this are mechanics and doctors. Mechanics work with oil, gas and other chemicals that are harmful to people and the environment. Doctors also work with biohazards such as other people's blood.

    o Buy the building and land or rent a building big enough for your business.

    o If you buy land and need to build, you need to know how much the land costs and how much it costs to build the store. If you rent a building, you need to know how much it costs to set up the store the way you want it. And, if you buy a building and land, how much it costs to remodel the building for your store.

    o If your business is only service – this means you are not selling things like toys or clothes, but are fixing something for people or installing things – you will need to know how much it will cost to set up an office space. Good examples of service businesses include lawyers, doctors and plumbers. Even though plumbers may sell things like hot water heaters, many times they buy the things they need from another store, then hook them up for you.

o   You will also need to know how much it costs to hire a lawyer to help you with the legal part of setting up a business. The legal part might include "closing" on the land and building – this happens whenever you buy property. This is a meeting between you and the person who is selling the property. At the meeting, you sign the mortgage and the person selling signs the deed to the property. The deed is the paper that says who owns the property.

o   Another cost is how much you need to hire a lawyer to help you with legal papers needed to start the business. To get a bank account and get the licenses you need, must have a business name. You can choose from a corporation, partnership, Limited Liability Company or several other types. Your lawyer will explain what the difference is and will tell you which kind of business is the best one for what you are planning. Each type of business has its own papers to fill out. Each also has its own way it is taxed by the Internal Revenue Service (I.R.S.).

o   If you are selling things such as toys, animals supplies in a pet shop, clothes or any other product, you will need to know how much to stock. This is called initial inventory. The first time you buy everything from a wholesaler – a person who sells things to stores – it is going to cost a lot of money. As you sell the things on your shelves, you buy more, but it's usually only a few things at a time. For the first year, you are going to have to guess at how much inventory you need. Your business plan will help you guess closer than if you just took a stab in the dark at it.

    o   If you are selling services only, you still need to figure out how much it costs for licenses, office space and equipment. If you have a plumbing repair shop, you may need two or three trucks for you and your employees, tools and depending on the type of services you offer, special equipment. If you are planning on opening a doctor's office, you need hospital beds and machines to tell you what might be wrong with people – diagnostic equipment. A doctor's office also needs office supplies, money to pay employees and supplies such as bandages and needles.

- Part of the business plan is determining whether the business will succeed. You have to guess how much money your business will make during the first five years. You do this by knowing how many cars drive by the business, how many people need to buy the things you sell, how many people need the service you might sell and how much you are going to charge people. For example, if you are selling clothes, then you have to know how much money you will make on each piece of clothing.

    o   If you are selling services – for example, legal services, you need to know how much to charge per hour. You also need to know how much you will be paying legal assistants, paralegals and, if you want to open a law office with other attorneys, how much you will pay them. On top of all of that, you need to plan to have computers, a network, Internet, and office supplies. Because attorneys have to go to court – they don't just sit in their offices – you will need to have a car for your business.

o   Things that you must think about include how much it costs to keep your store open every month and how much money you need for inventory. To figure this out, you add together how much rent or mortgage you pay every month, how much all your bills like electricity and telephone cost every month, how much you pay people who work for you and how much you need for inventory, supplies and other costs. Add all this together, and then divide it by the number of things you want to sell every month.

o   If that number comes out to $10 for 500 items, then you have to add that to the cost of each item. If you can buy a shirt from your supplier for $15, you'll have to add $10 to that amount. But, that will only allow you to make enough to keep the store running. You have to also add in enough money for you to make a profit. So, you should sell the shirt for no less than $25 if you want to make $10 profit to pay your own house bills and buy nice things for yourself.

•   Part of the business plan is deciding what you want to sell and to know who sells the same things you do. This applies if you sell products in a store or if you sell services. If you decide to sell clothes, list everything you want to sell – shirts, shoes, socks, pants, shorts and accessories. You will most likely want to sell different brands unless you are going to make everything you sell. List each type of clothing for every brand you sell because it might cost $15 for a Brand A shirt, but it might cost only $8 for a Brand B shirt. This means the price for everything that is different changes. You'll have to sell a Brand A shirt for no less than $25 to make a profit, but you can sell the Brand B shirt for $17 and make the same profit.

o   If you are only providing services, you have to go through the same procedure. But in this case, you may not have things to sell – at least not that you keep in inventory – but you may have extra costs for equipment. Add those monthly payments, along with the cost for the building and any other monthly costs together. Divide the cost by the number of service calls you expect to make to determine how many service calls you need to make to break even and how many service calls you need to make to make a profit.

o   The other thing you need to take into consideration is your competition. This means that no matter what you do – unless you make your own line of clothing – someone else is going to sell the same things or provide the same services.

o   When you look at the competition, you need what they charge for the same products or services you plan on selling. You should also watch to see how many customers they get; and what kind of customers. Are their customers mostly young mothers with children? Are they usually men? What age? This will give you a good idea of whom to send advertising to – someone between 18 and 35, someone between 35 and 55, or someone older. It also tells you if you should send advertisements to mostly men or mostly women.

o You should also know what your competition sells. If your competition sells Brand C shirt, you may want to sell different brands to bring people into your store. This is because you are offering something different from someone who already sells one brand. You can still sell some of the same brands, but when you choose something different, as long as it is a popular brand, people will come to your store.

- In the next part of the business plan, you will need to write out the strategy to reach your goals. In this section, you will outline how you are going to get people to come to your store or call you to fix their plumbing problem – or whatever service you decide to offer. This section also talks about your goals. For example, if you want to make $100,000 the first year, you write how you expect to do that by outlining your advertising methods, the number of people you expect to buy your things or hire you to fix something and how you can reduce the cost for initial inventory.

o Reducing the cost can be done by calling around to different vendors – people who sell the things you want to sell. As long as the less expensive product has just as much quality as the more expensive product, you can use it. When shopping for products, you have to keep in mind that sometimes you have to pay more to get better quality.

    ○ Mapping out the business model means you plan how you are going to do things throughout the first five years of business. This includes what you sell, how you sell it and how you advertise it. Customer service – how you treat customers – is very important and is a good part of whether your business survives or fails. This also means selling good quality products. If you sell something that breaks the first time someone uses it, they are not going to come back to your store to buy anything else.

- If you need to borrow money to get your business started, the business plan tells bankers, investors and partners all about your idea. It tells them how much money you have to help get the business started; and how much money you need to borrow to get it started. Think of the business plan as a long letter all about your business; and why and how it will succeed. This is how you get people to help you get your store or office open.

Where Do I Start?

Trying to create a business plan can be a little scary at first because you have to have so much information. You don't know where to start, especially if you've never written a business plan before. Even if you have written a business plan before, a different business needs different information, and it is still hard to know where to start. The rest of this book gives you some ideas of how to make a business plan that banks, investors and partners will read.

First Things First

Start by writing about yourself. Talk about your background – where you're from, what school you went to, what college degrees you have and plan on getting, what kind of jobs you worked in, and what you did in those jobs. Think about each job. Did you do anything special in any job that made work easier for you and others? Did you invent something new to help make your job easier? Did you write a computer program to help you and others in your job? Did you find a new way to do something? Don't be afraid to tell people about all the great things you've done. When you can show you have been successful, then people are more willing to help you get your business started.

The Next Step

Write about the things you want to sell. If you are selling items, discuss each item and why it is useful to people. Is there something different about your item that will make people want it more than someone else's item? Talk about the person or factory who will supply you with your initial and ongoing inventory. Write down how much each item is going to cost you. It's a good idea to create a full product description for each item you are selling. You can use the product descriptions on a web site later, and won't have to write them again.

If you are providing services, discuss the same things, but talk about your customer service – how you treat people. Also talk about why your work is better than everyone else's work. Maybe you came up with a great idea to make something easier or to make something work better. Maybe you invented a better widget. Tell the person who is going to read the business plan – usually the person from whom you want to borrow money or a person that might be your partner – about the widget you invented, what it does and how it helps people.

The final thing in this section is to talk about how your product is going to be produced. You may buy your product in bulk from a wholesaler. If your product is something you invented, you may want to build a factory to build the product, and then sell it your own store near the factory. You may decide to hire a factory to build your product for you if it's cheaper than making the product yourself. Whichever method you choose, be prepared to write about the cost of the method in the business plan.

Finding Customers

As stated before, you need to know who might be your best customer. While you may have many of one type, you will also get other types of customers. First, decide what age group might be most likely to buy your products. If you are selling clothes for children, your best customers might be female under the age of 35, but you may have males also buying children's clothes. You can't forget about the single parents or men who want to buy a gift for a relative. If you are selling clothes for sports, your best customers might be males and females from 16 to 45. If you are selling designer clothes, your best customers might be over 20 years old and make $100,000 per year.

You also have to determine how much money you can make off your products, and this is part of figuring out who might buy your clothing line. If you are selling children's clothes, most of your customers may not want to spend more than $15 to $20 per item or outfit. Yet, if you sell designer children's clothes, you want to advertise to parents who make more than $50,000 per year and who are under 35 years old.

As part of the business plan, make an outline of all the people who would be interested in your product, and how much money they make per year. Once you do this, you can look up the facts for your area – where your store is located – to see how many people who meet the criteria live near your store. For example, you would not want to sell expensive designer clothes in an area that has an average income of $25,000 per year.

Tell the Reader Why People Will Buy Your Product or Service

While you may have talked a little bit about why people would buy your products or services, fully describe why in this section. If you sell a better way to do something, describe your service and how your service is better than everyone else's service. A good example of this is paintless dent repair, a method that is not too old.

Instead of a person spending a lot of money to get a dented fender replaced, the person who provides paintless dent repair uses special tools to pop the dent out of the fender. In most cases, the paint is not destroyed, so the customer doesn't have to pay to replace the fender or repaint the fender. The process to fix the dent is not only quicker, but it is also cheaper than the regular way people fix fenders.

In some cases, the planned location of your store is closer to people who need your service. If you are lucky, you may open a plumbing shop, but the closest one to people who live near your new shop is 25 miles away. People will come to you just because you are closer – and you can make a very successful business as long as you provide the best customer service and offer a good warranty on your work.

Pricing

One of the most important parts of a business plan is the pricing of your product or service. Pricing shows a bank, investor or partner that you have planned this business with a lot of thought. It also shows that you know how much you need to make so you can pay the store's bills and employees.

Another part of this section is describing how you might talk someone into buying something more expensive or more than one thing. This is called up-selling. Also explain how many times a customer might buy something from you each year. If you sell clothes, you could expect to see a customer five or six time per year. But if you sell plumbing services, you might see the same customer once every year. This makes a difference in how you plan to advertise your products or services.

When you are completing this part of the business plan, you may have to do some research. You might look at government web sites to see how many people drive by your store, how much people who live in the area make every year and you might watch your competitors – those who sell the same products or services – to see how many customers they get every week.

Money to Start the Business

Once you have everything else figured out, you have to tie it in to show how much money you will need to start your business. List everything you need, plus the cost of each item. This part can get a little tricky, because you don't know how much money you need to buy a store front. Because of that, you will need to do some research on the cost of the type of building you want, and then you have to stick to your budget.

Location is going to determine how much you need to spend on property. If you are selling designer clothing you need to find a property in a part of town with a lot of traffic; and that traffic must be people who make a lot of money every year. If not, you won't sell very many things. You may have to wait to find the perfect location for your store.

Once you know what type of traffic you need, you can start checking prices for buildings that are perfect for your business. You'll then know about how much you have to spend to buy the right store front in the right place. This step is a little easier if you are going to rent a business, though monthly rent in a great location is going to be more expensive than rent in a location that is not perfect.

If you find buildings cost between $500,000 and $800,000 in the area where you want to put your store, list the higher amount in the business plan. If you are going to be renting, find out how much rent is in the area. Business rent is usually calculated by the square foot. If someone tells you the rent is $10 per square foot, multiply the amount by how many square feet you need. Use this number in this section.

Don't forget to list office supplies, equipment; and estimate monthly utilities such as electricity, phone, cell phone, water, septic and Internet. Figure how much you will need for the first year.

How Do You Know Your Business is Going to Succeed?

When you do a business plan, you won't get anyone to invest in your business unless you can convince them that your business is going to succeed. You will have to show proof of this. Proof might be another business's success, government reports that show how much traffic passes your store and government reports that show how much money people in the area spend on products or services like you are going to sell.

Creating a Summary

Because a business plan is so long, a summary is very important. The summary should talk about all of the important parts of the business plan, such as financing, why you think your business will be successful and why you think people will come to your store rather than someone else's store.

When you write the summary, it is the last thing you write because you are repeating things that you already stated. But, put the summary at the beginning of the business plan. Banks, investors and partners will read the summary before they read anything else to see if they want to read the rest of the business plan.

You should talk about everything except how much money you will need. When you get to the end of the summary, then you can add in the amount of money you need to start your business. As long as you make the summary interesting; your idea is something the reader might be interested in; and the idea sounds like it might work, you will have help getting your business started.

Chapter 7
Crisis Management for Beginners

Every company's worst nightmare is facing a public relations crisis. You can choose from many ways to handle a crisis, but if you choose the wrong way, it could cost your company dearly, especially a publicly traded company. As soon as the media gets wind of something that went drastically wrong, the stock could drop.

Once stock starts dropping and people start selling out, you end up with a vicious circle: People sell because others are dumping the stock as fast as possible. Meanwhile, the stock and your reputation continue to fall as more people sell. You can avoid this scenario by following certain steps to avoid a PR crisis or handling a crisis in the proper manner.

Even a small private company can fall victim – word of mouth travels quickly, and you'll notice sales dropping off if you don't appropriately manage the PR crisis.

Be Prepared to Handle a PR Crisis

Inevitably, a PR crisis is going to happen at some point in a business's life. You can minimize the damage by being prepared. You should know what risks your business has – use these risk factors to create a PR crisis plan by anticipating things that could go wrong. Once you have a list, create questions that you think the media and individuals may ask. Once you have the questions listed, you can create answers to the questions.

For example, if you manufacture food and one or more of the ingredients are outsourced, there is a risk of using tainted ingredients in your product. You can minimize this risk by using only fresh, quality ingredients that meet U.S.D.A. standards. If something does happen, you can tell people that your ingredients meet standards and that you are taking steps to ensure that tainted ingredients do not enter your factory. Steps may be as drastic as changing suppliers.

When you have the answers ahead of time, it is easier to face the media and others who have questions regarding the crisis. Furthermore – and more importantly, if you have prepared responses, everyone who speaks to the media will have the same response.

Prevent a PR Crisis from Happening

Even though you can minimize the damage of a PR crisis by having responses ready, it is best to prevent a crisis from happening. No matter how much you minimize the damage, you are still going to lose sales. By knowing your company's risks and closing vulnerable holes, you can prevent a PR crisis. For example, if you import a certain ingredient from another country, then learn that the country's food regulations are not as strict as the U.S. regulations, you can change suppliers.

Respond Quickly

If you do find yourself on the wrong side of a PR crisis, be sure to respond to questions within 48 hours. If you think you can ignore the situation and it will go away, you are sadly mistaken. People will be posting on social media faster than you can imagine. Once the first person "shares" the issue, it's out there, just like a big pink elephant in the middle of your living room. By responding to questions quickly, you do not give the public or media a chance to infer things that may not be true.

Have the Right Attitude

If you look at the crisis from a journalist's point of view, you look for facts. Is the PR crisis caused by someone who was harmed or by someone who holds a grudge and wants to damage the company's reputation? Before you make a statement, be sure you have all of the facts.

If a person is not telling the truth about a matter and you try to rectify it in an incorrect manner, you could give the impression that the lies are true. At the same time, if a person is telling the truth, he or she could stretch the truth to a point where it could excessively damage the company's reputation.

Be sure to respond to the situation in a timely manner so others don't have time to come to their own conclusions. If you do have to go on a fact-finding mission, tell the public and media that you are still investigating the problem and that you will update them as soon as you know something.

Don't Allow Doubt

Once you have all of the facts, you can speak professionally and intentionally to your audience. Make sure you are clear on what you say so there is no room for interpretation. Word each statement so that it cannot lead to questions that you may not be prepared for. The public and media are great at twisting things to suit their purposes. If your answers are wishy-washy, you open the door for rumors and doubt about your statements.

Keep Your Staff Up to Date

Make sure your employees know how to respond to certain questions. If you have a small group of employees, this is easier as everyone can prepare the same answers. However, if your company is a large manufacturing plant with hundreds of employees, you may want to instruct all of them to refer the media and others who ask questions to the department heads. The department heads can answer questions, but you should still tell your employees what is going on even though you instruct them not to speak to the media.

Employees who are not in the know tend to make things up just like the media and the public. Don't allow this to happen by keeping all employees informed of the situation and what you are doing to rectify the problem.

Contact the Affected

One of the most important things you should do to minimize a PR crisis is to call the affected people. At the very least, write a letter that is personally signed – not stamped – by you. Writing a letter may be better if a large group of people were affected by the problem.

Explain how the problem happened and what you are doing to keep it from happening again. Be prepared to speak to the affected person's attorney. Depending on the ramifications, which could be anything from embarrassment to the death of a loved one, the affected person may sue you or simply request a refund.

Assign Each Employee His or Her Own Responsibilities

Each department head should answer questions that pertain only to his or her department. If someone who works in the section that mixes pudding tries to respond to a question regarding packing and doesn't know anything about the packing process, that person could further damage the company's reputation and damage the steps taken to rectify the situation.

If the media or public asks a question that an employee should not respond to, instruct that employee to refer the questioner to the appropriate person.

Outside Assistance

Depending on the size of the problem, you may want to consider retaining a PR professional to help you minimize the problem by instructing you how to respond to the media. If you've never had to deal with a PR nightmare before, you may not be prepared to respond to certain questions in a manner that makes the company look responsible.

If you also retain attorneys that are not familiar with your process, make sure the attorneys are completely filled in on everything they need to know, including operating procedures, the situation that caused the PR crisis and what you are doing to rectify the situation.

Use the Crisis to Further Business

When you have a PR nightmare, your company is in the public eye. You may be on the television news, and at the very least, written up in the newspaper. Use this opportunity to explain the problem and how you are going to rectify the issue. You can also talk about other products and services that you have. A popular gas company did an excellent job of this after the fiasco in the Gulf of Mexico.

Be sure to also tell the public and media what you are doing to compensate those who require compensation for injuries or the death of a loved one. Be sure you don't promise anything you can't back up. The number of people affected will dictate what you can promise unless you have extremely deep pockets.

Always Have Something to Say

Never say "no comment." Saying this shows the media and the public that you may have known about the issue and didn't rectify it before it harmed someone. If you don't know an answer, tell the media that you are still looking into the situation. It is better to say that you are still looking at facts and circumstances than to give the impression that you have something to hide.

As soon as you get the information required to respond to the question, contact the person and give him or her the answer. At the same time, be prepared for additional questions that may be related to the original question.

Know and Understand Your Company's Past

As part of ensuring that a PR nightmare doesn't creep up on you, research your company's past if you were not there from the inception of the company. If something happens that causes a PR crisis, you will need to know how to respond based on previous happenings. You will also know what previously happened so that you can ensure that the proper steps were taken to keep a particular situation from happening again.

Reassure People

During the PR crisis, be sure to keep the public and media up to date on the steps you are taking to ensure the problem will not happen again. While you may not be able to guarantee that it won't happen again, you can ensure people that you are taking steps to hopefully prevent it. An example would be if an ice cream packing machine broke and a piece was found in a customer's gallon of ice cream.

You can let people know exactly what happened and the steps you are taking to prevent something like this from happening again. You may tell them that you decreased the time between machine inspections or that you implemented another process to scan the product to ensure the packaging has not been damaged.

Media Training

Before you have a crisis you and your employees should attend media training. You will learn how to be comfortable speaking to the media so that it is harder for it to read something negative into what you are saying. Media training also teaches you to know the reporter and what types of questions a particular reporter may ask. It also teaches you to know how long to speak to the media. Sometimes, if you allow it, the media will hog all of your valuable time with question after question.

Create Crisis Response Team

Creating a crisis response team before a crisis happens is one of the best ways to avert disaster. Appoint people – preferably at least one person from each department – to the team. The team will create a plan to respond to and rectify a PR crisis. Your team should have media training and know how to answer questions about all aspects of the business.

With a crisis response team, you and your employees don't have to worry about responding to questions – you can refer everyone to the crisis response team. The team would be trained to respond to any PR crisis at any time and can act quicker, thus minimizing damage.

Summary

When you first take an executive job with a company, check into its history and find out whether the company has a crisis response team. If not, you should consider putting a team together, attending media training and getting ready to answer any question thrown at you.

Furthermore, be prepared to rectify a bad situation immediately. Whether a machine needs to be replaced, people need to better adhere to a dress code or safety regulations or quality control needs to be amped up, you should have a plan to ensure that the action that caused the crisis doesn't happen again.

Chapter 8
Taking Your Company Public and Creating a Solid Corporate Structure

Before you take a company public, you must complete up to 14 steps to set up the company, including offering its stock on one of the public trading markets and filing appropriate documents with the Securities and Exchange Commission. The action of trading the stock among other things happening within the company and the economy dictate the price of the stock. All of these things affect your venture's worth in the financial realm.

Selecting the Board of Directors

Normally the shareholders elect a board of directors, but when just starting a company, you have to create your own. You should choose a chief executive officer and a chief financial officer, plus others depending on the size of the company. If you have never run a company before, you should hire someone with extensive experience as a CEO or you could run your company into the ground before it creates the first sale.

When you have more than two members on the board, you have the benefit of getting additional advice, adding experience to the company and accountability. Furthermore, if you choose the proper members for the board, you could have legal counsel, plus you will have relationships with other like-minded business people.

You are the founder. The other two or three people are those you trust to help run your company. Choose carefully as you may want another founding member, plus one investor who is not a founding member. The founding members should always have control of the company. If you have two investors and they both require a seat on the board, increase your board to five members. Three of you will be founders and the two investors are not, thus you keep control of the company away from the investors.

A nominating entity, the person – or people -- with control over the company, nominate additional directors as you need them. Once nominated, the shareholders vote the potential directors onto the board.

Selecting a Board of Advisors

Even with a board of directors, you may want a board of advisors. When you create a board of advisors, chose three to five people who can benefit your company with their knowledge. If you use less than three people, you won't get enough advice, but if you use more than five, you have too many people giving you advice. When you have too much advice coming your way and you try to take everyone's advice, you end up hurting the company rather than improving it.

Furthermore, you need to limit the term of service for the board of advisors. Because it is difficult to tell people you don't need their advice anymore or to let someone go if that person doesn't "mesh" with your company, it is best to limit service to six months. If you really like one or more of your advisors, you can offer to renew their term on the board for another six months.

Choose advisors that have experience with your business. It is best not to ask professionals such as lawyers and accountants; instead ask those with experience in your products or services. Also, you should be sure the people you ask have experience in growing a company. If you want to grow to a multi-million dollar company, don't ask an investor who has experience in growing a multi-billion dollar company. As your company grows, you can take on different advisors; and when you are ready to move from a multi-million dollar company to a multi-billion dollar company, that is the time to ask for someone with that experience.

Selecting and Qualifying C Level Executives

C Level executives are high-ranking executives and are often on the board of directors. You may be the chief executive officer or CEO; and you may have several other C Level executives, including but not limited to:

- Chief Compliance Officer or CCO

- Chief Security Officer or CSO

- Chief Financial Officer or CFO

- Chief Information Officer or CIO

- Chief Knowledge Officer or CKO

The C Level executives you choose should be well-qualified in their specific areas, especially if you decide to vote them onto the board of directors. When looking for the right person, locate someone who has branded themselves. Branding links a person's strengths, key personal attributes and passions. These are the things that will tell you whether your choice in a C Level executive is what your company needs to succeed.

The person you choose should stand out from everyone else when you look at his or her entire package. Most of all, the person should have extensive experience in his or her field. For example, a chief security officer should have years of experience within all aspects of IT security and a chief financial officer should have extensive experience within the financial community, including working as a certified public accountant or a forensic accountant.

Identifying Strategic Alliance

A strategic alliance is when companies partner to create products and do it without actually merging into one company. The companies meet with a neutral mediator before they strike a deal. They learn the weaknesses of the agreement before they sign anything, which means the issues are corrected to make the contract stronger. The parties are less likely to enter into a lawsuit because of a disagreement or a violation of the contract.

An example of a strategic alliance is a wine company that doesn't grow its own grapes. The wine maker partners with a grape farmer to buy the grapes. In some cases, partnering with someone to produce some or all of the ingredients required allows you to create a product that is less expensive but has better quality.

You can create a strategic alliance with more than one company. For example, if you are selling a specific brand of screwdrivers, you may partner with a company to make the shaft; and partner with another company to make the handle. Your company would put the two together and sell the screwdrivers.

Pre-Public Expansion Strategy Identification and Facilitation

Before you go public, you should also have an expansion strategy in place, along with methods to put the strategy to work for your business. This involves figuring prospective income and debt, which should also be part of your business plan.

Growth is important to a successful business and you should plan ahead of time for that growth. As you get more orders, you will need more employees, even if you partner with other companies for support in product development and manufacturing.

Furthermore, you will need to advise partner companies of your growth as they will need to produce more. Growth of your company may include opening satellite offices if you offer services, additional factory space, or adding strategic alliances. Regardless of how you plan to increase production, you must have the income or must be able to obtain the financing to facilitate the growth of your company.

Business Plan Authoring

Before you can get financing for your business, you need a business plan. You can draft your own, but it is better to retain a company experienced in creating them. The business plan author will ensure that every part of the plan is complete with up-to-date statistics, graphs and tables.

The length of the business plan depends on your company and where you plan to take it. You may have a 20-page business plan for a small boutique business, a 50-page plan for a manufacturing company that plans to stay in one area, or you may have a 100-page business plan for a company that plans on going international and has several strategic alliances.

Business plans tell potential investors and partners that you have done your homework regarding making your business successful. This means that you chose a great location, know how you are going to pay your employees and how you are going to expand. It also shows demographics such as daily traffic (potential walk-in customers), how you are going to entice customers into your establishment and how many sales you expect to make per month and per year, among many other things.

Private Placement Memorandum Authoring

If you are not planning on taking your company public right away, you can still offer stock. You do not have to register the stock; however, you do need to create a private placement memorandum. The private placement memorandum tells prospective investors about your company's finances.

You may be able to grab investors' interests without a private placement memorandum, but because an investor is giving you quite a sum of money at an already high risk, chances are, you won't get an investor without disclosing the company's financial information.

A private placement memorandum tells potential investors several things, including:

- Certain restrictions and requirements imposed upon investors

- Special notice

- Several summaries, which are outlined in detail later in the Private Placement Memorandum

- Investor suitability standards

- Risk factors

- Strategic planning information

- Management team information

The risk factors delineate the risks involved with investing in a private company, including losing the entire investment. The management team tells potential investors about the management team. The strategic planning information tells investors what you plan on doing with the money they give you to grow your company.

Public Company Accounting Oversight Board Audit

The Public Company Accounting Oversight Board is a nonprofit corporation that was established by Congress. The Board protects the interests of investors by overseeing public company audits, including compliance reports filed under federal securities laws and broker-dealer audits. It also provides independent audit reports.

The Securities and Exchange Commission has approved several standards (referred to as AS numbers) related to auditing companies, including references in auditors' reports, internal control audits, quality review, audit planning and audit risk.

The Board also adopted several standards that already existed. These are the Board's interim standards, which include the responsibilities of an independent auditor, professional care and illegal acts among several other standards.

Public accounting firms must be in compliance with the Sarbanes-Oxley Act and the rules of the SEC in addition to professional standards in connection with the issuance of audit reports and the performance of audits. The Board conducts annual inspections of firms that provide audit reports for over 100 issuers. For firms that provide audit reports for less than 100 issuers, the Board completes an inspection at least every three years.

The Board must provide the SEC with a written report on every inspection, plus it makes a part of the reports available to the public. The Act also requires certain information to be withheld from the public, and that information is not included in the reports. Some information may be held and provided at a delayed date in accordance with the Act.

S-1 Filing

The S-1 Form is required by the Securities and Exchange Commission if you are taking your company public. If you have securities that meet the SEC's requirements, you must file the S-1 Form before you can list the shares on a national exchange.

In addition to filing an S-1, you must provide additional items to the SEC, including the prospectus of the planned security, any dilution because of other listed securities, and your methodology of the offering price. The company must also disclose any business dealings between the company and outside counsel, and between the company and its directors.

The S-1 Form discloses how many shares the company is offering and the price per share. The S-1 Form also outlines the risks involved to the investor.

Also included in the S-1 Form:

- Industry and market data

- A section detailing what you will use the money for

- The company's dividend policy

- Capitalization

- Dilution

- Financial data

- The management's analysis of the company's financial condition

- What the company is going to pay its executives

- Relationships and other party transactions

- A list of the principal stockholders

- The description of the capital stock

- The number of shares that are eligible for future sale

The purpose of the S-1 Form is to disclose information about the company to potential investors.

15c211 Filing/FINRA Trading Symbol

Once a private company has completed all other requirements to go public, it must file a 15c211 application with FINRA to get a trading symbol. One of the requirements is that the company must have at least 35 shareholders. Once a company receives its symbol, the Market Maker can quote the company's securities on the open market and trade them on the Over the Counter market.

The 15c211 filing is called as such because SEC rule 15c2-11 governs the actions taken by a company to get a symbol. After the market maker quotes a company's securities for 30 continuous days, other market makers are eligible to quote the securities.

Post Public Investor Relations Solutions

One of management's responsibilities is investor relations. You could have a separate investor relations department or your public relations department could double up. Investor relations integrate communication, finance, securities law compliance and marketing so that two-way communication between the company and others, including the financial community, is open. Ultimately, the information contributes to the valuation of the company's stock.

The investor relations department usually reports to the chief financial officer or the treasurer. The U.S. Department of Labor qualifies investor relations as a specialty branch of public relations.

Investor relations often oversee press conferences, shareholder meetings, meetings with investors, annual reports and the investor relations section of a company's website.

The investor relations department also works with the corporate secretary on regulatory and legal matters that may affect shareholders. In addition, it must be aware of issues that relate to organizational impact, fiduciary duty and other upcoming or current issues.

Promotion and Building the Corporate Brand

Before you can go public, you must also have a corporate brand. The brand is how potential investors and customers identify you and your products and/or services. When someone sees your brand, that person or entity identifies it with your reputation -- in a nutshell, how you treat customers, plus the quality of your products and/or services, define your company and could mean the difference between success and failure.

Once you start promoting your brand and people start purchasing your products and/or services, you start building your reputation. While excellence is commanded in the first few years of business, you should not slack off. Everything that happens is associated with your brand. For example, if you have an employee who is having a particularly bad day and at least one customer is not happy with treatment by the employee, that customer is going to tell others to avoid your establishment. This could happen whether your business is one day or 100 years old.

Post Public Acquisition Identification

Identify any properties or other companies you may want to purchase after your company goes public. This should also be part of your business plan, specifically the part that discusses future growth. You must know what you want, even if it is not available yet, as well as your budget for this project.

When writing about post public acquisition, you don't just say you want to expand by guessing. This must be a well-planned strategy move, which means you are able to take a good guess as to the future success of your company. In other words, you can't just say you're going to buy out Company X if you don't know whether you can financially afford it.

Part of your business plan discusses future revenue and how your company is going to achieve that goal. With that in mind, you will be able to show how you will acquire post-public acquisitions to grow your company.

Post Public Subsidiary Mergers and Acquisition Identification

You often hear the terms "merger" and "acquisition" in one phrase. An acquisition is when one company buys another company. A merger is when two companies come together to create a bigger and better company.

As with acquisitions, mergers should be planned well ahead of time. If you are a new company that outsources, you may want to partner with a company to do away with the outsourcing. If you can merge with an existing company and integrate your structure and the new company's structure into one, you may be able to save more money than if you were to continue outsourcing or buy a company.

Another benefit of a merger or an acquisition is the increase in stock value. When a company buys or merges with another company, the action is seen as favorable because the company is successful and stable enough to participate in such a large transaction. When a company shows stability, the value of its stock rises.

Summary

Proper planning before you even start your business, or at least before you go public, not only gives you a better chance to succeed, but it also shows prospective investors that you have properly planned the future of your business.

With a proper business plan, branding and documentation, you can take your venture from an idea to a multi-million dollar company over time. Public trading, mergers and acquisitions also help with company reputation and growth. Complete all steps of building a company from the ground up; and don't forget that things that may seem small could have a large impact on the future of your company.

Furthermore, be aware of all rules and regulations of any agencies. If you plan on going public with any business, you must follow the rules as outlined by the SEC. You may also be subject to audits, and in any case, if not, keep in mind that an audit also helps investors make an informed decision about whether to invest in your company.

Because there are many steps to taking a company public, it is best to create a list of everything that must be done. The list will guide you through the process and ensure that you have not forgotten a step. If you are unfamiliar with any of the documents required, you should retain a professional to ensure that you do not waste money by filing the wrong documents.

Chapter 9
Different Kinds of Capital

Depending on how a business is set up, it could have up to five types of capital. Capital is the money you put into the business. In general, capital is assets that the business owns such as cash, machinery, real estate, accounts receivable and inventory. It takes money to buy all of these things to get a business started – that money has to come from somewhere, whether you put it in yourself, you borrow it or you get vendors to stock your shelves and allow you to pay for items as you sell them.

Don't think of capital as just cash – it is the amount of financial resources the owner has to execute his or her business plan. You need capital to develop a product, for sales and marketing, the legal formation of the company, administrative support, and to purchase real estate and inventory.

Equity Capital – Owner or Venture Capitalist Funded

Equity capital is the most understood form of capital. It is the net worth of the business and is figured by subtracting the liabilities from the assets. It is also more favored than any other type of capital since it is difficult to go into bankruptcy. Some sources say it is impossible to go bankrupt, but if the business falters and you must sell the equipment to pay the bills, you won't be able to continue manufacturing. You'll avoid bankruptcy, but you won't have the equipment to continue operating.

If you have a business that does not require a lot of capital to start, it is very difficult to go bankrupt in the event of a major financial catastrophe such as a major recession. For example, a sole proprietor attorney may invest $20,000 to start up, which includes renting his or her office, purchasing computers and office supplies, utilities and hiring a paralegal. If the business slows, he can simply lay off the paralegal and do the work himself. The chance of losing everything – unless he has no new clientele – is slim to none.

When you use equity capital, it takes a lot of work to grow a business, but if you can generate returns that are high enough, your business can have a pure equity capital structure instead of a combination of this and other types of capital.

When a business is funded with only equity capital, the owners and/or shareholders put in all of the cash and there are no liabilities offsetting the assets. The owners do not usually set terms for the company to pay back the equity, but instead, have a right to the future earnings. Owners may be paid with distributions or dividends as long as the company is profitable and has enough cash flow. Yes, the owners are paid last.

If the owners do not have the cash to support the execution of their business plan, they can enter into an agreement with a venture capitalist, who invests the capital under certain terms and conditions. The venture capitalist agrees to a percentage of future earnings, conversion rights or to hold a spot on the board of directors instead of repayment.

A venture capitalist does not receive payments on his or her investments, thus you will most likely have to provide a business plan that outlines your future financial picture. The investor will complete due diligence before making the investment, and that includes determining whether the business will survive long enough to make the investment worthwhile. The only way a venture is worthwhile to a venture capitalist is if it will pay more over time than the investor would have received if had loaned the money to the business owner.

Your business plan should show what other money you will be investing in the venture, how much profit you plan for each sale, how many sales you anticipate per day, month, quarter or year, and how you plan on attracting more customers over time.

Debt Capital – Interest Only Loans

Debt capital is also a popular way to fund businesses, simply because it is relatively easy to get. A business borrows money from a bank, a wealthy person, or bondholders and pays interest on the money. The business does not pay anything on the principal. The parties sign a contract stating that the business will pay the principal back on a certain date. The borrowed money is the capital and the interest is the cost of debt. You may have heard such loans being referred to as interest only loans.

Profits are realized after taxes and interest payments. For example, if you borrow $100,000 at 10 percent interest and earn 15 percent after taxes, you have a 5 percent profit.

Furthermore, the interest payments are tax deductible while the dividends paid on equity capital are not. Debt capital also allows a company to continue making a profit indefinitely as long as the company makes a high enough return to cover the interest payments.

The disadvantage of using debt capital is that the interest payments must be paid on time. With equity capital, if the money is not there, the owners do not get paid, and there are no consequences. Should the company lose sales, whether because of the economy or any other reason, it has to find the money to pay the interest payments or the lender can recall the loan.

Before a company decides to use debt equity, it must take a hard look at the economy and other factors that will financially affect the company. The best way to do this is to create a business plan. Furthermore, most investors will require the owner to submit a business plan as part of the investor's due diligence. It is very difficult to get debt capital without a business plan that outlines the business's anticipated growth over a five-year period.

As with obtaining equity capital through a venture capitalist, you must show anticipated profits and traffic flow. If the investor does not think your business plan is solid enough to show enough profit to pay the loan, the investor will deny funding.

Specialty Capital

Some forms of capital – negative cash conversion and float capital – have very little economic cost associated with it. These forms of capital allow your company to grow unheeded. Sweat equity is another form that has very little economic cost associated with it, but if you consider that time is money, it does have more cost than negative cash conversion and float capital. Your only limitation is how many hours per day you are willing to put into your business. Businesses generally grow faster if you can secure – or at least partially secure – at least one type of special capital.

- **Negative Cash Conversion or Vendor Financing**

  o   Negative cash conversion is also known as vendor financing. If you can get vendors to front you inventory, your initial capital investment will be significantly lower. The best way to understand negative cash conversion is to compare it with consignments.

  o   The vendor stocks your store with its products. You do not pay the vendor until you sell the product. As soon as you sell an item, the vendor sells it to you. You must then pay the vendor for the item you sold. Your contract with the vendor may be on a weekly or monthly basis. The vendor may also require you to pay for the sold items after you sell a certain number.

o   If you can get a vendor to stock your store without upfront payment, you can carry much more inventory; and this allows you to build your business much quicker. You won't have to worry about ordering an item that is too expensive to keep in inventory. Furthermore, negative cash conversion allows you to expand your business – to a larger store or to multiple locations – much quicker than if you had to buy more inventory.

o   Negative cash conversion also allows you to generate more income than other types of capital. You can measure vendor financing by comparing the percentage of inventory to the percentage of accounts payable and by reviewing the cash conversion cycle. When comparing percentages, the higher the percentage, the better. When you analyze the cash conversion, more negative days are better than positive days.

o   If you plan to use negative cash conversion as a form of equity, be sure to outline this in the business plan. Furthermore, you must show the investor how you are going to obtain enough sales and retain customers to make it worthwhile to stock your store with inventory. Many vendors will not allow you to stock without payment unless you can show that you will sell a certain number of units in a set amount of time.

- **Floating Capital – It's Not Your Money**

  o You've heard the sayings that "time is money" and "don't use your own money to start a business." Floating capital combines those two sayings for one of the best forms of capital – if you can make it work.

  o Floating capital is income that is generated and invested before you have to pay it out. The best example of a floating capital business is an insurance company. The insurance company collects money from people for insurance policy premiums, and then invests the money. It can do this because it does not need to pay out the money right away.

  o A person may pay his or her insurance premiums for several years before the insurance company needs to pay out on a claim filed by that person. Basically, floating capital is money held by a company, but not owned by the company. In some cases, the cost of capital is negative. In other words, the small cost of floating capital is offset by income from investments.

  o While this type of capital works great for insurance companies, it is very difficult for other types of companies to develop floating capital. Floating capital can also bite you in the butt. For example, if you provide home insurance and a hurricane wipes out most of your customer's homes, you'll have to pay out on every one of those policies. If you don't have enough return on your investments or you can't liquidate the investments, you won't have enough to pay the claims.

○ Your business plan should outline contingencies should Mother Nature – or another destructive force -- decide to wreak havoc on your financial stability.

- **Sweat Equity**

  ○ Sweat equity is not really a form of capital in the sense that there is no upfront cash, and most of it is intangible. However, time is money, thus the owner's time can be considered as capital. Generally, the owner puts in long hours at little to no pay. Since he or she doesn't have to pay someone else to do the work, the owner saves quite a bit of payroll expense and tax.

  ○ Sweat equity can work in many different situations. In the initial building phase, if the owner does some of the construction himself, he or she can get a discount on a general contractor's fees, since that is one less person the general contractor needs to pay. If the business is up and running and the owner works in the store, that is one less person he or she has to pay.

  ○ You often hear the term "sweat equity" associated with building a personal home, but it can be used in any situation where the owner can put in the hours instead of paying someone else to do the work.

  ○ For example, if a retail salesperson gets paid $10 per hour and works 40 hours, the owner saves $400 per week. Additionally, the owner would have to pay payroll taxes for the employee, worker's compensation insurance and other costs associated with payroll. These costs could easily add up to a couple hundred per week, especially if the owner provides health insurance for the employees.

○ Before you enter into a sweat equity agreement, be sure you understand the terms. Also, be sure that the contractor properly discounts his services. You are not gaining anything if the contractor would normally pay a carpenter $50,000 per job but only discounts his fee by $10,000 in exchange for your hard labor.

Summary

The type of capital you use depends on your current financial position and the type of business you are starting. If you created a new invention and planned to manufacture it yourself, you will need a ton of capital to purchase the manufacturing plant, the equipment and machines, and all of the "small things" such as office furniture and supplies. In a case such as this, you may use a combination of equity capital, debt capital, sweat equity.

If you are opening a retail store you might use equity and debt capital, plus add some sweat equity and negative cash conversion.

When you draft your business plan, you need to keep the types of equity in mind so you can determine whether you need to borrow. If you need to borrow (debt capital), you will need to show the investor – via the business plan – what you expect out of the business for at least five years.

The investor will want to see demographics, how many sales you plan to make per month and how you intend to get the sales. He or she will also need to see your profits. For example, if you are selling an item, how many do you have to sell so that the profit covers the payment to the investor and the operating expenses such as payroll, utilities and the mortgage or rent.

You'll find advantages and disadvantages to all types of capital. When deciding your business structure and financial plans, you may consider all types of capital, but be sure to use the type that best benefits your business. You could even use a combination of several types of capital to best benefit your financial picture.

Chapter 10
What is Stock?

All corporations have stock. When you own stock in a company, you own a piece of the company; and stock is used to keep track of who owns the company. For example, if you own 1,000 shares and that company has 10,000 shares, then you own one-tenth of the company. Stocks are also referred as shares of a company and you will sometimes see them referred to as "shares of stock."

Investors can trade shares if the company is publicly traded. This means that the company registers its shares of stock on the stock market. Anyone can buy shares and sell shares. If you buy at the right time and sell at the right time, you can make money by trading stock. The value of the stock changes based on the company's actions.

Private and Public Companies

Public companies are registered which makes it easy to buy and sell their stock. It allows you to own a part of the company without you having to do any work for it; or be involved in its operations. You can sell your stock any time you want.

Private companies, usually small businesses, might have stock, but it is not publicly traded. Only a few people have access to the stock; and generally, you have to be invited to purchase private stock; and this is also very risky. Also, you can't just sell stock in a private company. There is usually no market for it because the stock is not registered. If the company does register the stock, it may be very difficult to sell it because different stock markets may not want to list it.

How Does Owning Stock Benefit You?

When you buy stock in a company, you are called a shareholder in the company. There may be thousands of shareholders in a company depending on its size and the amount of stock the company has registered. When you own stock in the company, you are entitled to three things:

- If the company pays dividends – a portion of their profits – to the shareholders, every shareholder gets the same amount of money for every share he or she owns;

- If the owners of the company sell the company or the assets, you as a shareholder, are entitled to part of the money the company makes on the sale. When a company sells assets, this is called "liquidation." This means it turns assets into cash by selling them; and

- You are allowed to vote for people to be elected to the company's board of directors. The board of directors of a company is responsible for running the company. Some companies instruct the board of directors to hire people to run the company instead of running the company themselves.

Since voting rights do not have much value the value of the stock is determined by two things:

- Future Dividends: A future dividend is how much the company expects to earn.

- Earnings and Assets: This is how much the company is worth should the owners sell the company.

Why Should You Invest in Stocks?

The biggest reason people invest in stocks is to make money. It is also the easiest way to own several businesses. When you own several businesses, you benefit from the profits of the company while doing no work for the company. You can also invest in mutual funds. One mutual fund owns stocks in several companies – even thousands of companies. You could buy shares in a mutual fund to further increase the ability to buy into more companies and decrease risk.

The risk involved is that a company could lose money. If the company loses money and the price of the stock drops, you lose money on your investment. For example, if you buy 100 shares of stock in Company A for $100 per share, your cost is $10,000. If the value of the company's shares of stock increases by $1, your profit is $100. If the value of the company's shares of stock drops by $50, you just lost $5,000.

Values could rise and fall several times per day. This is what makes trading stock risky. A company's stock could drop by $10 in the morning but it could increase by $20 at the end of the day. It is up to you to guess whether the stock will increase or decrease, as this tells you when you should sell.

If you ignore daily fluctuations and plan on holding onto the stock for at least 10 years, you are trading based on the long method approach. Generally, if the company is profitable most of the time, you will make more money than you would if you invested in bonds, savings accounts, real estate or certificates of deposit.

Since you don't have to watch the stock market daily to see how your stock in individual companies is trading, you save a lot of time. Mutual funds are excellent for the long method.

Getting Started with Options

Most people don't buy individual stocks. Rather, they invest in mutual funds so they can buy parts of many different companies. This reduces the risk involved in the investment. One of the biggest benefits of owning mutual funds other than they are less risky is that you can invest a smaller amount of money to cover more companies. In other words, instead of investing $1,000 in one or two companies and hoping they don't fail, you can invest the same $1,000 in a mutual fund that has several hundred companies with a lot less risk of the mutual fund failing.

Investing through a mutual fund means you "diversify" your investment. You own stock in several hundred companies instead of one or two, so when one company does fail, you won't lose as much money. Investing over the long term also reduces your risk. Because one company's stock falls today doesn't mean that it won't come back or even increase its worth in the future.

When you see news about stocks on television, you often see news about one or two stocks that happen to be doing very well at the time. This might entice you to invest in one or two stocks, but this would be a mistake, especially if you are investing for a short term. Studies have shown that people who invest in only a few companies do not do well in the stock market.

When you diversify by investing in many different companies and preferably through a mutual fund -- you tend to make more money on your investments.

Picking the Right Stocks

Once you decide whether you want to invest in individual stocks or mutual funds, you have to decide which stocks or mutual funds in which to invest. Some people think you have to pick a specific industry, but you are mistaken.

Instead, you should research the companies to see how it manages its operations and finances. If the company is well-organized and makes good money, then this is a company you might consider investing in. Companies that are registered to sell their stock must provide investors with their financials. It would be a bad move to invest in a company that is and has been in debt for some time and has a hard time bringing in any money.

Most companies have debt so you can't base your decision on the amount of debt only – you have to look at monthly and/or yearly profits. The more time a company shows growth, the less risk you have with your investment.

Factors in Sorting Stocks

You should look at three different things when deciding which you want to invest in: Stock valuation, stock size and stock geography.

- Stock Size: The size of the stock is calculated by determining market capitalization. Market capitalization is the total value of all of the company's outstanding stock. To find this value, multiply the share price by the number of shares of existing stock. If a company has 10,000 shares of stock and each share of stock is worth $100, then the market capitalization is $1,000,000. Companies are sized in three categories:

  o Large Cap: A company with more than $10 billion in stock.

  o Mid Cap: A company with $2 billion to $10 billion in stock.

  o Small Cap: A company with less than $2 billion in stock.

Larger companies are usually less risky to invest in because they generally have more security. Security means that a company has a lot of revenue – money from sales, can take loans with less interest and have more products than smaller companies. When a company is stable, the price of its stock does not go up and down as often as the stock of a company that is less stable.

When you invest, it is a good idea to have a portfolio with some large cap stocks, some mid cap stocks and some small cap stocks because sometimes the small cap stocks make more than the large cap stocks.

- Valuation of the Stock: Stocks are divided into three valuation categories: Value stocks, core stocks and growth stocks. Growth stocks grow faster but are riskier.

  o Growth Stocks: Companies with growth stocks are believed to have more earnings in the future. The price of these companies' stocks are based on what the companies could make in the future, not what they are making right now. A good example of this is a new line of clothing that is expected to be the new trend. If the company doesn't grow as expected, then you could lose a lot of money. That is where the risk comes in.

  o Value Stocks: When stocks are sold as value stocks, their value is lower than what they should be based on the company's assets and income. A company's asset value is figured by adding together all of the company's assets including incoming cash (receivables) minus the company's debt. Companies with value stock are generally having a hard time financially or is losing business.

- Core Stocks: A core stock doesn't fall into growth or value stocks. The company with core stocks is not fast growing nor is it losing money.

- Balancing Core, Value and Growth Stocks: If you are investing for the long term, value stocks may be the better option. These companies may have a comeback in months or a few years. Growth stocks may grow for a short time, then stop growing. When choosing a portfolio, you should have a good combination of core, value and growth stocks if you are investing for the long term.

  - If you can buy stocks while they are cheap and wait until they grow, you will make more money than if you were to buy stocks then almost immediately sell them. You may want to shy away from value stocks, but these companies could come back after a tough time. Buying these stocks at a discount – buying low – affords you more profit when the company recovers.

  - Don't forget, a growth stock might make you good money in the near future. But, if you are investing over 10 or more years, these stocks could end up making you less than if you were to buy a stock that steadily grows little by little every year or a value stock that might grow by leaps and bounds over the next five or ten years.

- Stock Geography: An investment portfolio that is well-balanced should also include international stocks. A company that is not in the United States also has stocks. Because the company is out of the country, these stocks are called international stocks. International stocks feature two different types: Developed market and emerging market.

- Developed Market: A developed market stock is much like stocks in the United States. The country where the company is located has a stable economy and government. Companies in countries such as Germany, Japan and the United Kingdom are developed markets.

  o Emerging Markets: An emerging market is the market of countries which were once known as third world countries. These countries' economies and governments are new and growing. When you invest in a company in an emerging market, you are taking more risk because the country's economy is not stable. Also, companies in an emerging market may not have good financial reporting, thus increasing the risk of stock in these companies.

When you add the value of all the stocks in the developed markets, they are a bit higher than the total worth of stocks in the United States. When you add the value of all the stocks in the emerging market, they are worth only about one-quarter of what all the stocks are in the United States.

Risks in International Stocks

In addition to the risk with emerging markets, you have one more risk – currency risk – that comes with investing in international stocks. This risk comes with investing in developed or emerging markets. This is because you depend on the worth of other countries' currency – for example, Euros or Japanese yen. Since you change your U.S. dollars into the local currency, then back again, the value of the dollar figures into the stock value. If the Euro is worth $2 U.S. dollars the day you buy the stock, but is worth $1.50 U.S. dollars when you sell the stock, you take a $0.50 loss.

You can avoid large drops in income by investing in an international portfolio of many stocks instead of investing in a few individual companies.

Foreign Stock Market Indices

A stock market index tells you how your stocks are doing. The United States has several; and the most common are Standard and Poor 500 – often referred to as the S&P 500 and the Dow Jones Industrial Average. Foreign stock also has indexes to tell you how your international stock is doing. A common international index is the MSCI-EAFE. This is comparable with the S&P 500 and includes companies in Asia, Europe and the Pacific.

With this information, you can make a better decision on the type and amount of stock you want to buy, or whether you prefer to invest in mutual funds or a combination of individual stocks and mutual funds.

General Rules for Investing

When investing, do your research before plunking money down. You may want to invest in mutual funds or a combination of mutual funds and individual stocks. Regardless of what you choose to do, be sure to keep in mind that value stocks are usually better for long-term investing; smaller companies mean you assume more risk than investing in larger companies; and international stocks have their own risks and benefits and should be added to your investment portfolio. When you have an investment portfolio, you have many different stocks and/ or mutual funds. Most of what is in your portfolio should be long-term investments.

Buying Stocks

Now that you have decided what type of stocks to invest in, you have to buy the stocks. You could invest in a mutual fund through a retirement plan, an investment account or a brokerage account. A brokerage account is opened with a brokerage firm. The firm could be a full-service firm, an online firm or a discount firm. If you're still not sure about your investments, you can always hire a financial advisor to help you with investment advice.

The cost of the brokerage firm varies from firm to firm. In most cases, you'll have to pay a commission to the brokerage for each trade. Also, in most cases, you need the funds up front to buy stocks. Some brokerage firms will allow you to pay later – but not much later. You might have to deposit the funds within three days of the trade.

A full-service firm is usually quite a bit more expensive, as these firms cater to higher-wealth investors. These investors often need help picking the right investments. An online broker or discount broker is a lot cheaper to work with.

Buying Mutual Funds or Exchange Traded Funds

Many people learn about picking mutual funds when they set up their retirement plan or Individual Retirement Arrangement (IRA) accounts. For those who are not using a full-service brokerage firm, it might be better to start with mutual funds as they are less risky and offer long-term investments. Many different companies, including brokerages, offer mutual funds.

Regardless of what avenue you choose to purchase mutual funds, be sure to research companies before signing up with them so you find the company that works best for your situation. Some companies have a list of mutual funds that you can buy without paying a transaction fee. These are called no-load mutual funds. Be careful, as no-load mutual funds often have other costs associated with them that could make the cost of owning them more expensive than if you were to buy a mutual fund with a transaction fee or commission.

Exchange Traded Funds

An exchange-traded fund is similar to a mutual fund, but it is traded the same way stocks are traded. You can purchase an ETF from any discount or online brokerage house if you don't need investment advice. Before you pick one online or discount brokerage, check their commission rates as they vary.

Things to Consider Before Choosing a Brokerage Firm

Before you choose a brokerage firm, also check the firm's money market rates if you plan on keeping cash in your brokerage account. Choose a firm with a better interest rate, as the higher interest rate is usually bigger profit to you than a smaller trading commission unless you plan on trading often.

If you plan on purchasing your initial stocks, mutual funds or exchange traded funds and sitting on them for several years, you'll do better with a firm that offers a higher interest on cash in your account; and if you plan on trading more often, you'll do better with a firm that offers a lower interest rate on your account, but offers a lower commission on each trade.

You can also check with credit unions, banks and savings and loans as many have brokers available to you. These places may charge a higher commission, but it could be worth it if the brokers give you advice about buying and selling.

And last but not least, be sure you pick a firm with a good reputation. A firm with a bad reputation could lose all of your money. If that were the case, you could invest yourself and lose the money on your own.

Summary

Before you make an investment, be sure to choose whether you want to invest in stocks, mutual funds or exchange traded funds. When you invest in stocks – whether individually or via mutual funds or exchange traded funds – you are buying a piece of ownership in a company. If you are investing in individual companies, you can choose companies with different valuations, companies in different countries, companies in developed or emerging companies, companies whose stock is expected to grow fast and even companies who are in financial trouble.

Since it is best to invest in many different types of companies over a long term, you might consider investing in mutual funds. Mutual funds could have from several to thousands of companies. Because of this, your investment risk is lower than if you were to invest in several individual companies.

Investing in mutual funds not only allows you to invest in and own pieces of many different companies, but it also allows you to own more companies for less money, and allows you to have a more diverse portfolio.

Advanced Section

Chapter 11
What is an S1?

S-1 is the preliminary registration form for new securities requisite by the Securities and Exchange Commission (SEC) for public companies. Any offering that complies with the criteria must have an S-1 filing before the shares get listed on a national exchange.

Form S-1 necessitate companies to make available information on the planned use of capital proceeds, explain the current business model and competition, as well present a concise prospectus of the planned security itself, along with submitting price methodology, and any dilution that will occur to other listed securities. The SEC also requires the revelation of any material business transactions between the company and its directors and outside counsel.

Form S-1 is also known as the Registration Statement under the Securities Exchange Act of 1933."

Investors can access the S-1 filings online to perform due analysis on new offerings earlier to the issue. The form is sometimes modified as material information or general market conditions cause a delay in the offering.

The Securities Exchange Act of 1933, often referred to as the "truth in securities" law, requires that these registration forms are filed to unveil essential information upon registration of a company's securities. This assists the SEC to accomplish the objectives of this act, which is requiring investors to obtain important information on the subject of securities offered, and to proscribe fraud in the sale of the offered securities.

A relatively easy registration form is the S-3, for companies that do not have the same ongoing reporting requirements.

All companies can use Form S-1 to register their securities offerings. A registration statement cannot be prepared as a fill-in-blank form, like a tax return. It is more like a brochure, providing legible information to the public. In the S-1, a company must explain each of the following in the prospectus:

- Its business;

- The plan for distributing the securities;

- Its properties;

- The identity of its officers and directors and their compensation;

- Its competition;

- Material transactions between the company and its officers and directors;

- The intended use of the proceeds of the offering

- Result of Operations

- Certain relationship and related transactions

- Market for common equity and related stockholder matters

- Executive compensation and Indemnification of officers

- Expenses of issuance and Distribution

- Material legal proceedings involving the company or its officers and directors;

- Recent sales and unregistered securities

Information about how to portray these items is set out in SEC rules. Registration statements also must comprise financial statements audited by an independent certified public accountant.

Apart from the information specifically required by the form, the company must also endow with any other information that is essential to make the disclosure complete and not ambiguous. Company also must clearly express any foreseen risks in the prospectus, usually at the beginning. Examples of these risk factors are:

- Lack of business operating history;

- Adverse economic conditions in a particular industry;

- Lack of a market for the securities offered; and

- Dependence upon key personnel.

Various offerings, which can be done using the Public sale of free trading stock form S-1 are

- Initial Public Offering

- Direct Public Offering

- Selling stockholder offering

- Private Investment in Public Equity or PIPE

- Equity Line.

Another Form S-8, also called a registration statement, comprise information provided by a company to SEC, if the company plans to register securities earmarked for employees under the firm's benefit or incentive programs. The S-8 document is concise and hassle free, as long as the material facts about company's intent to register company securities tied to benefit plans are comprehensive and detailed. The basic differences between S-1 and S-8, S-1 requires quite a few to be filled, providing details of firm's decision to go public, while S-8 asks for a little detail. Completing S-1 form is a difficult task and takes a long time, considering information gathering, but Form S-8 facilitate companies to register shares quick and easy. Form S-1 must be accompanied by multiple chapters and hundreds of pages of data, while S-8 Form, which generally is a 10 page document, rarely exceeds 20 pages of documentation.

Chapter 12
Why Entrepreneurs Use Private Placement Memorandums

A document which comprises relevant disclosures so that investors can measure and get to know the risks involved with an investment and make a fully informed decision for the investment is known as Private Placement Memorandum (PPM). A formal PPM is made to fulfill all the disclosure requirement of Rule 502(b) (2) of Regulation D. The rules, though, take under their jurisdiction only certain type of investment which have non-accredited investors, almost every private investment where one solicits more than few investors will need some form of disclosure documents.

Private placement memorandum can at times have some variation in terms like "Confidential Information Memorandum" or "Disclosure Document", but these are all essentially PPM.

A PPM does not have any specific form. It is based on the type of company which wants to disclose the information to investors. Though there are usually some boxes that need to be checked, regarding disclosure, but the form and information are a company and deal specific. There is a need of Financial, accounting and legal expertise to design a private placement memorandum.

Several ways can be adopted by a company to offer a private placement memorandum.

- **Attorneys**. There are firms who approach an attorney to prepare the private placement memorandum. After the designing of PPM is complete, management of the company is responsible for soliciting and approaching the potential new investors. The cost incurred is the fees of the attorney who designed the PPM and the time spend by the management team. Preparing a PPM through an attorney can be a good option for companies' that already have a well-built network of potential investors to pitch the investment opportunity.

- **Investment Banks**. The firms can also hire a liaison to assist in raising capital. This can be tricky, confusing, and time consuming. When an entrepreneur works towards raising capital, he/she approaches all sort of institutions offering all kinds of promises to raise money. This can certainly go wrong and confusing. The entrepreneur should be vigilant and informed to hire a right investment bank as one wrong step can kill the company.

- **PPM Specialists**. Firms specializing in this arena are often a hybrid between legal counsel and an investment bank

Why Private Placement Memorandum?

The PPM should be nice and updated document abiding by all legal requirements because through this document the company is showcasing its best picture to investors, disclosing all risks and other information. The PPM should also be professional, providing all the legal disclosure.

PPM is required to make investors aware that the entrepreneur is seeking to fulfill the applicable SEC rules. Another reason for designing PPM is to add some additional protection to entrepreneur and the company. The private placement memorandum document is drafted to detail the risk factors and more so that investors while reading the offering memorandum will understand the company's risks. This is important if the company raising the capital ends into bankruptcy. Private placement memorandum is thus a guarantee to the entrepreneur that the investors were aware of all the risk that the company may or may not see in the future. Private placement memorandum serves as the warning to the investors of the risk integrated in the investment and also helps to protect the seller of the security.

The memorandum provides details about the business, background information on management, details the terms of offering (including the number of shares available, the price, and the intended use for the funds), an overview of the company's capital structure prior and after the sale of securities, discloses the opportunities and risks pertaining to an investment and presents copies of financial statements.

At times, law does not makes written disclosure mandatory, the statement of the issuer still needs to be in compliance with the federal and state anti-fraud requirements. The issuer should not make false claims and immaterial facts to the investor. If investor comes across any such material misstatement, irrespective of it being unintentional, investors may file a securities fraud claim against the issuer, and if needed against its directors and officers, as well.

Further, the Securities and Exchange Commission (SEC) can enforce civil and criminal penalties, too. A well-prepared PPM helps to keep away a securities fraud claim. It creates the record of every communication which was made to the investors regarding the offering and the company.

Chapter 13
What is a Direct Public Offering?

Direct public offering implies that the company raises capital by issuing it shares directly to its own suppliers, distributors, employees, customers and friends in the community. These are an alternative to broker-dealer firms.

Direct public offerings are significantly less costly than traditional underwritten offerings. DPOs also don't carry restrictions that are usually stringed to the bank and venture capital financing.

Prerequisites of filing

- **Preparation of the Prospectus.** The official offering document is known as Prospectus and is incorporated in the registration statement filed with the SEC. It is inclusive of all details related to company.

- **Reporting and Disclosure**. All the reporting and disclosure requirements should align with the offering else it would be considered as the violation of state or Federal law.

- **States' Regulatory Issues**. The DPO must be registered in every state where the company wishes to sell stock. While most of the states accept a form U-7 for the filing, yet many states have different and/or additional regulations and filing fee structures.

- **Subscription Agent**. The agent is required to ensure the company's compliance with varying state restrictions. Care should be taken to avoid penalties.

- **Accounting**. An audited financial statement may be required depending on the nature of the offering. Any licensed CPA can provide such services.

- **Attorney**. To complete the offering in full compliance, an attorney will be needed.

- **Financial Printing**. There are certain documents, like the printing, inventory and delivery of stock certificates; safeguarding unissued certificates, etc, required for the offering.

Fund obtained from DPO

From the theoretical perspective, a company can raise a large amount of money from direct public offering, but that is not the case in practical due to organizational limitations involved in achieving that level of stock sales.

Currently, the maximum limits, which can be raised using various forms of the Direct Public Offering, are:

- SCOR (Reg D) -- $1 Million

- Regulation A -- $5 Million

- SB1 -- $10 Million

- SB2 -- $25 Million

Benefits of DPO

The expense part for direct public offering, when compared to initial public offering is less. There are no underwriters in direct public offerings because they are issued through officers and directors. Unlike an IPO, the shares in DPO are directly marketed to parties that may be interested in the company stocks, and the buyers generally include customer, distributor, or employees.

There are companies which are not very large and cannot get the benefit from the initial public offering. Direct public offering is an attractive alternative to them. Many consider the biggest advantage of a direct public offering is the fact that capital raised doesn't have to be paid back. Corporations can give up a share of the company for the funds it requires. Often, those funds are obtained with far less intensity than what could have been expected with a venture capital firm.

Often the company finds it more suitable to raise funds through a direct public offering than through a traditional debt financing like a bank loan. This turns out to be true where the business involves high risk that involves little physical capital that could be used as security. A direct public offering enables the corporation to market it to those who are more capable of understanding and bearing the risk.

Drawbacks

Although Direct Public offering enjoys various benefits it has few drawbacks. The process is not straightforward, and an immense deal of information is to be collected to prepare a registration statement to file with the SEC. Similar to an initial public offering, a direct public offering can deflect the concentration of employees for many months. The difference between the costs of DPO and IPO is not very much. In DPO though the money is not spent on underwriters but a part of that will be invested in marketing efforts.

Federal Government consideration

The Security and Exchange commission is the historical federal regulator of Public offering activities, and it allows individual states to regulate securities offerings under $1 million.

The last major problem linked with being public a company was the reporting requirements. In 1992, the SEC's Small Business Initiatives simplified the reporting rules and minimized the costs of compliance with federal securities laws.

Chapter 14
Advantages and Disadvantages to a Direct Public Offering

A direct public offering (DPO) is a financial tool that facilitates a company to offer stock directly to investors—without using a broker or underwrite as a mediator—and avoid certain expenses related with "going public" through an initial public offering (IPO). DPO is a form of exempt securities offering, which implies that companies choosing this form of offering are not liable to many of the registration and reporting requirements of the Securities and Exchange Commission (SEC).

DPOs first became accessible to small businesses in 1976, but they only attain recognition starting in 1989, when the rules were made simple. The small business initiative program was started by SEC in the year 1992 which eliminated even more hurdles that limited the ability of small companies to raise money by selling stock. In the recent years Internet has enhanced the use of Direct Public offering a lot. In fact, around 200 small companies in the latter half of the 1990s went public via this route, either by directly offering their stock online or through their web sites or by listing with one of the several online DPO forums.

A DPO falls into one of three regulatory classes:

Regulation D: this is the most popular form of DPO; a regulation D also called Small Corporate Offering Registration

(SCOR) enables the company to raise up to one million dollars every 12 months. Shares are registered with state's securities regulatory administration.

Regulation A: enables a company to raise up to five million dollars annually. However, Reg A DPO mandates registration with the Securities and Exchange Commission's Small Business Office. This escalates the costs of compliance and reporting, and adds another agency monitoring every 90 days.

Intrastate DPO: there is no upper limit on the amount of the fund which can be raised, but the fund must be raised within the states.

Advantages

A company going for a DPO is adding equity by attracting new shareholders from the public. There are more than one reason why DPO is an increasingly popular alternative for growth oriented micro and small business.

- A DPO is less costly to the company when compared to an IPO.

- The regulatory burden in case of DPO under Regulation A is comparatively minimal.

- The SEC has encouraged the use of the Internet for DPO's.

Generally when there are high expectations from a company to attract venture capital, then the venture capital firm generally asks for stake and/or substantial amounts of equity. In some cases, the entrepreneur loses control of his or her company and can be removed. The Direct Public Offering is a potential alternative to IPOs and venture capital. DPOs enable the owner of the aggressive companies to raise funds that they need without sacrificing control on their corporations. The costs, which are associated with the DPO, are far more manageable and rational.

For investors, it is also a smart investment alternative. The investors hardly have access to venture capital investment, and thus they cannot access the rate of returns that those investments can bring. Thus, the DPO method is advantageous for both investors and entrepreneurs.

Disadvantages

The amount of money, which a company can raise through DPO in any 12 month period, is restricted by regulations.

Arriving at a market price is difficult because DPO is not issued and traded publicly like IPOs and thus it may require regular valuations of the company assets, both realized and unrealized.

Administrative and legal necessities for creating and maintaining a DPO are noteworthy, and divert company resources from expansion initiatives. The costs of creating and staying in compliance with DPO requirements may cost more than the company has to pay for expansion capital.

Meeting state or SEC requirements can be difficult, time-consuming and expensive.

Sufficient funds are hard to raise through DPO.

Any company should ask and take the suggestions of the tax attorney or the chief financial officer about the cost of creating and maintaining a compliant DPO before taking the step and work those numbers over and again to create the best and worst case scenario. This gives any company the better picture of the value of the DPO to business, both for short and long term.

Chapter 15
What are the differences between the OTC.BB and Pink Sheets?

The OTC Bulletin Board is a network of many market makers, with each reporting current bids, offers, and completed trades to a centralized computer.

Pink sheet is a daily publication accumulated by the National Quotation Bureau with bid and asks prices of over-the-counter (OTC) stocks, including the market makers who trade them. The Pink sheets got their name because they were actually printed on Pink paper. The Pink sheets were initiated as a daily quote service provided by the National quotation bureau.

Stocks of small companies are generally traded on both OTCBB and Pink sheets. The stocks on both the OTCBB and Pink sheet are traded over the counter, but there is a significant difference between both the markets.

The companies usually suffering from two aspects are traded on OTCBB. The first aspect is that the company is delisted from the major stock exchanges. The company may be going through harsh times and fails to meet the listing requirement of the NASDAQ or NYSE then it will be delisted. It can also happen when the company is undergoing financial crisis. The other type of companies is small companies failing to comply with the listing requirements of the big stock exchanges. These two types of companies, however, need to meet some listing requirements of SEC filing and minimum requirements set by the OTCBB.

On the other hand, contrary to the OTCBB, companies having over the counter stocks traded through Pink sheet market do not need to fulfill any minimum requirements. Most of the stocks offered by these companies come under the criteria of the penny stocks.

Unlike OTCBB, companies on the pink sheets are hard to analyze because it is gruesome to get accurate information about them.

One major difference between Pink sheets and OTCBB is that, Pink sheet is owned by Pink sheet LLC, a private company, whereas OTCBB is owned by FINRA, a self-regulatory organization. However regulation and operation, of both, do not go through any major changes because of the change in ownership. The regulation over both the markets is done by FINRA's regulation of conduct of brokers-dealers that submit quotes in each facility.

The Pink link service of Pink sheets in particular provides participating broker-dealers with the better method to achieve compliance with their best execution obligation contrary to OTCBB system.

The reason why OTCBB cannot accept quotes in securities that are not part of a class of securities registered under Section 12(g) of the exchange act is that FINRA, which owns the OTCBB, decided in 1999 that it was not suitable for the OTCBB to do so. As a result, Pink Sheets accepts quotes in securities that are part of a class of registered securities, as well as in securities that are not registered while the OTCBB will only accept quotes in securities that are part of a class of registered securities.

One of the major benefits to OTCBB over the Pinks is that if one sees a continuing quotation showing on an OTCBB stock that means it is currently undergoing regulatory filings—a necessary element to remain listed. If the company is late in filing, an 'E' is fixed to the quote symbol until the company completes its regulatory filings. Failing to do so within the 30-60 day grace period, the security will be removed.

One particular trend, which is proving to be beneficial for growing listing on Pink sheets, is the prohibitive cost and regulation associated with the OTCBB or any other exchange. More and more companies are inclined towards Pink sheets in their initial stages or formative stage. The list of ever increasing regulatory requirements is just too troublesome for smaller companies.

It is fairly possible that most of the investors never had a chance to hear or deal on the pink sheet world a few years ago, but with the advent of the Internet, its visibility has improved to a point that issues and volumes have increased exponentially. While this may be a supplement to the 'legitimacy' of the Pink Sheets, investors need to be very careful because the Pink sheet companies do not require any regulatory filings and usually do not open their financial status, in front of the public, unlike OTCBB.

Chapter 16
What is a Blank-check Company?

A blank check company is a development stage company that has no definite business plan or purpose or has laid out its business plan to connect in a merger or acquisition with an unidentified company or companies, other entity, or person. These companies in general involve tentative investments and come under the SEC's definition of "penny stocks" or "micro cap stocks".

The companies are called the blank-check companies because this is what they get from the investors—a blank check for the company to select any (or no) targets for take-over. Since this is a blind-faith gesture, investor confidence depends on the status of the company principals.

The SEC prohibits the blank-check companies to use some of the exemptions from the registration requirement when selling their securities. The Security and exchange commission do so because of the nature of the blank-check companies.

If a blank check company registers for the security offering it should comply with some additional requirements for the protection of the investors, including depositing most of the raised funds in an escrow account until an acquisition is settled, and it requires shareholder approval of any identified acquisition.

"Special purpose Acquisition Company or SPAC" is a type of Blank Check Company. A SPAC is established specifically to raise funds in order to finance a merger or acquisition opportunity within a limited time period.

The Securities exchange commission has laid out some rules for the blank-check companies. At least 80% of the total shareholders' money should be utilized in all the acquisitions, and each acquisition is subjected to shareholder approval. If the company fails to find or execute at least one transaction by a given date (generally two years from inception), the funds plus accrued interest less operating expenses are returned to the shareholders.

Most of the blank-check companies issue initial public offerings of around 10 per share, but they can also raise funds without the approval of shareholders by issuing other class of stocks. So many companies do this to keep them safe from hostile takeover. Some of these companies have more than one class of preferred stock, and it's not easy if not impossible to differentiate one from the other. One of the major problems which arise in researching such area is that there is little to no information on the blank-checks which very well explains their thin trading volume.

There are about sixty to hundred blank-check companies trading on the US exchanges. The major player's, trade on AMEX.

The Blank check companies can succeed in for what they have been formed only when all hopes turn out into the final result. Management should be able to find an appropriate acquisition candidate and settle a bargain price. Operators must run the enterprise well. The stock market must shore up a rising valuation for the acquired company. But these factors seldom coincide.

Generally among all the factors one or two go wrong. Either the company fails to find a willing target and returns the money to investors or if everything goes on the track at times the company overpays for the acquisition, leaving IPO investors with big losses.

Since 2003, a total of 98 U.S. companies were set up to form such special-purpose acquisitions, according to SPAC Investments Ltd. The average annualized return of such so-called SPACs has been negative 18.4% in the stock market since 2003, against an average of 6.7 percent for the Standard & Poor's 500 Index.

The past records of the blank-check companies are full of scandals, and U.S. regulators have time after time made tougher rules on how these businesses operate. One of the rules says that the acquisitions can't advance without shareholders consent. Managers are prohibited from paying themselves huge and excessive fee before they have done any work or gamble away IPO earnings in ways that shareholders wouldn't welcome. These rules safeguard the U.S. investors to a large extent and should also be followed by other countries'.

In order to regulate the blank check company in the most effective way, such offerings should be off-limit to anyone except to the sorts of wealthy investors who by now participate in hedge funds and private equity. These kinds of rules will be important and efficient to safeguard the blank-check deals that allow perilous foreign companies to trade on U.S. or European exchanges without fulfilling usual listing requirements.

Global capital markets already make available ample of different ways for the best corporate acquirers to pursue their craft. At a time when more transparency and disclosure are critical to rejuvenate public confidence in the markets, the intrinsically opaque nature of the blank-check companies strikes a dissonant note.

Chapter 17
SEC Rules for Cyber Security Disclosure

In May 2011, Senator Jay Rockefeller requested to the Securities and Exchange Commission that it should advice public companies on the time when disclosure of cyber security risk to investors is compulsory. On October 13th, the Division of Corporate Finance at the SEC issued a Disclosure Guidance that for the first time advises registrants to evaluate their cyber security risks and if found necessary these risks should be disclosed to investors. The companies which ignore the suggestion of Division of corporate finance and fail to disclose important cyber security risks do so at their own risk and are liable to regulatory and legal action.

Irrespective of their area of business, be it banking retail or defense industry, companies are facing diverse array of cyber security risks, on a daily basis, from the cyber criminals who attempt on stealing the important and vulnerable information or corrupt data.

Overview of the disclosure guidance

The SEC staff states that its Disclosure Guidance is "consistent with the relevant disclosure considerations that arise in connection with any business risk." The disclosure regulations say that SEC is aware of the fact that detailed cyber disclosure could compromise cyber security issues. In this regard, the SEC rules do not require disclosure that would compromise a company's cyber security. Instead, it states that companies should "provide sufficient disclosure to allow investors to appreciate the nature of the risks faced by the particular registrant in a manner that would not have that consequence."

The Disclosure Guidance concedes that existing SEC disclosure rules do not openly refer cyber security matters but states that such revelations may still be mandatory under existing SEC rules. Important information in connection with cyber security risks and cyber incidents are required to be disclosed as and when necessary, to ensure other required disclosures are not misleading in light of the circumstances under which they are made.

The cyber security disclosure is similar to SEC 2010 interpretative release in accordance with SEC climate change disclosure. The Disclosure Guidance makes available the SEC staff's thoughts on the application of existing SEC disclosure rules to cyber security matters. Particularly, the Disclosure Guidance addresses disclosure contemplations appropriate to both cyber security risks and cyber incidents under the following provisions:-

Risk factors

Risk factor disclosed under Item 503 should comprise a discussion of cyber security and cyber incidents if such issues are one of the most important factors that make an investment in the company perilous or tentative. The risk factor disclosures of cyber security should be made according to the individual company's facts and circumstances and should keep away from "boilerplate" disclosures.

Management's Discussion and Analysis (MD&A) of Financial Condition and Results of Operations

Under Item 303, the MD&A should comprise a discussion of cyber security risks and occurrence if cyber incidents are probably capable of leaving an impact on company's liquidity, results of operations or financial condition or would cause reported financial information not to be essentially investigative of future operating result or financial condition.

Description of Business

The cyber incidents should be discussed by the public companies in their Business description if these incidents significantly impact a company's products and services, relationships with customers or suppliers, or competitive conditions. The disclosure should encompass the impact of the cyber incidents on each reportable segment.

Legal Proceedings

If there is any pending legal proceeding involving a cyber-incident in which the company or any of its subsidiary is a party to the litigation, companies need to disclose about that legal proceeding.

Financial Statement Disclosures

Cyber security risks and cyber incidents may have major effects on a company's financial statements. Companies should make sure that any such impact to financial statements is accounted for pursuant to applicable accounting guidance.

Disclosure Controls and Procedures

It may be possible that a cyber-event might disturb the company's capacity to provide the SEC with the information necessary to be disclosed on SEC filings; in such case the company may conclude that its disclosure controls and procedures are futile.

Chapter 18
Capitalization table

A private placement memorandum should have the capitalization table because it is a significant part of the document. It gives the detail about the shareholders of the company and shows their corresponding ownership shares including their voting rights and other specifics. If the issuer is a sole proprietor then, the capitalization table will not be required as the owner is the 100% owner of the company. But if the company raise money from investor, he or she shares the ownership of the company and thus the Cap table is required. Cap tables are helpful for public companies for paying out the dividends from profitable operations and/or divvy up the windfall after the owner sells the company.

A cap table is basically complex and includes various calculations and a reference to other numbers. It can be represented in various layouts and formats.

Pre-Money and Post-Money Ownership

This table is used for the purpose of the issuer to better understand how the percentage ownership will change with the current capital raising program of the issuer. The understanding of the cap table is crucial for the issuer if the raising of funds results into original owners losing the necessary 50% of voting rights, which give the issuer control of the company.

If the issuer raises the smaller amount and spend more time in making its business plan successful with the limited amount of financing, the company can avoid losing controlling interest in the company both now and in the future round of financing.

Common, Preferred, Options, Warrants

The cap table should specify clearly the difference between common stock and preferred stock. The preferred stockholders generally have no voting right but are paid dividends before common stockholders. The issuer should raise preferred stock in order to keep control over the company which is not possible with raising equity shares. Investors, however, who have knowledge of the investment, prefer the equity share with which comes the controlling that gives the voting right. Such investors would like to invest in equity stock if there are voting rights instead of dividend in preferred stock.

Warrants that have been issued or those, which are due to be issued, should be included in the cap table. This helps the management and the prospective investors a get a fair picture of the likely future changes in the ownership, if and when the options or warrants are executed.

Chapter 19
Advantage of Listing on the FSE

The Frankfurt stock exchange is one of the biggest trading centers of the world, and there are over 3000 US companies listed on it. The brutal Sarbanes Oxley Act introduced in United States in the year 2002 has led North American and other foreign companies to Choose Europe over the United States.

The Deutsche Borse owns and operates the Frankfurt Stock Exchange other than FSE; it also owns the European futures exchange Eurex and clearing company Clearstream. It is the largest of all German stock exchanges, responsible for approximately 90 percent of the securities trading volume in Germany.

Advantages of Listing on FSE

Xetra is the latest and most versatile trading platform in the world. The Xetra platform continuously scans the market to match buyer and sellers at a faster speed compared to the New York stock exchange's platform. It lets faster alert detection such as irregular buying and selling patterns tapped in the market. More than 90% of trading is now done through Xetra with a fifth of them placed by private investors. Companies can be sure of fair pricing, low costs (no brokerage fees), tremendous speed with fastest execution times, broad selection with over 6,000 securities, and flexibility on order execution. Today, a total of 260 market participants in 19 countries are linked to the system. At peak times, Xetra processes up to 1.4 million trades per day.

The benefit, which Frankfurt stock exchange allows, is ease, speed to market, and low cost when it comes to listing a company. The audited financials are not needed along with the assets or revenue requirements, which grant ease of entry to the companies. The time needed for getting listed on FSE is as little as 12 weeks, and the approximate cost incurred is $70000.

Other advantages, which a company enjoys by listing on Frankfurt Stock Exchange, are the relaxed regulations that allow U.S. listed companies to avoid the grueling load of the Sarbanes-Oxley Act that U.S. public companies must stick on to if they're listed on a U.S. Exchange.

European investors can buy shares of the North American company in their local currency if the North American company gets listed on Frankfurt Stock exchange. It also helps to establish a more acknowledged presence of these companies in Europe and Asia. The company gets access to over 100 million people in Germany, Switzerland, Austria, and Liechtenstein by getting listed on FSE.

European investors wanting to invest in Canadian and American companies pay higher brokerage fees if they have to buy the stock on the North American Market.There is a huge drop in the fee if the European investor opts for buying from Frankfurt stock exchange instead from North American stock exchange. The fee drops by almost one-tenth of the original fee, thus providing the European investors cheaper and easier trading conditions for Canadian and U.S.stocks.

The company gets the stability by listing on Frankfurt stock exchange. It enhances the company's public perception. This is the key to providing a company with the resources and ability to expand the company, as well as raise capital. The company gets noticed by the more affluent retail and institutional investors, searching the European and other financial websites, to help make their investment decision.

For investors in any stock exchange, transparency is the extreme important criteria. At Frankfurt Stock Exchange, there are three levels of transparency. First is Prime Standard, second is General Standard, and third is Entry Standard.

Frankfurt stock exchange has greater access to capital. It has access to 1/3 of the total investment capital in the world. Frankfurt Stock exchange gets huge exposure to investor capital with more than 250 international trading institutions and over 4500 traders worldwide.

Naked short selling is prohibited in the Frankfurt stock exchange. Germany passed this regulation in June 2010. Critics and experts said that the short selling was a major cause behind the US market downturns. Short selling is a technique where the investors or short sellers manipulate the market by selling the securities which they actually don't have. This act leads to manipulation in the market.

Frankfurt stock exchange is an internationally acknowledged stock exchange just like NASDAQ or the New York stock exchange. The liquidity of stocks listed on the FSE is the greatest in all of Europe, including London and Paris stock exchanges. Market liquidity and trading volume of Frankfurt Stock Exchange is number three in the world, behind only to NASDAQ and NYSE but without their listing requirement.

Fastest rate of growth, the highest earning per person in the EU and the strong Euro are some reasons why companies are looking forward to get listed on Frankfurt stock exchange rather than on the NASDAQ, Bulletin Board, or Pink Sheet.